Maynooth Research Guides for Irish Local History: Number 4

Pre-Census Sources for Irish Demography

Brian Gurrin

FOUR COURTS PRESS

Set in 10.5 pt on 12.5 pt Bembo by
Carrigboy Typesetting Services for
FOUR COURTS PRESS
Fumbally Court, Fumbally Lane, Dublin 8
e-mail: info@four-courts-press.ie
and in North America by
FOUR COURTS PRESS
c/o ISBS, 5824 NE Hassalo Street, Portland, OR 97213

A catalogue record for this title
is available from the British Library.

ISBN 1–85182–619–X

Printed and bound in Great Britain by
MPG Books Ltd, Bodmin, Cornwall

Contents

Illustrations and tables   6

Abbreviations *and* Useful libraries and genealogy societies   7

Acknowledgements   9

Introduction   11

1   Pre-census demographic analysis in Ireland   14
        A brief history of pre-census Irish population estimation   14
        Pre-census substitutes   23

2   Sources for pre-census population studies   25
        Current thoughts on Irish demography   25
        Census substitutes   27
        Pre-census population sources – poll-tax summary, 1660   30
        Pre-census population sources – the hearth-tax   36
        Pre-census population sources – religious censuses   44
        Pre-census population sources – estate surveys   56
        Pre-census population sources – church records   60
        Miscellaneous sources   64

3   Researching pre-census demographic sources: some problems and
    possibilities   68
        A multiplicity of multipliers   69
        Verifying census data   79

Conclusion   88

Appendices
        A. Hearth-money county farm totals   89
        B. Available hearth-tax rolls and summaries   90
        C. Template for recording baptisms   95
        D. Estimating the proportion of farmers and labourers from
             the 1660 poll-tax returns   96

Select bibliography   99

Illustrations and tables

FIGURES

1	Sample page from 1660 poll-tax summary	31
2	Sample page from 1666–7 hearth-roll for County Tipperary	39
3	Sample pages from Malton estate survey, County Wicklow, c.1730	59

TABLES

1	Provincial population and house estimates for 1706	16
2	Religious breakdown estimates for 1731	18
3	Housing-stock estimates for 1732	19
4	Distribution of Protestants and Catholics between provinces as reported by the 1731 and 1732 'censuses'	20
5	Typical structure of data presented in the 1660 poll-tax return	32
6	Revenue in county rolls compared with county farm totals for 1672 and 1682	41
7	Comparison between pre- and post-amendment hearth-rolls	42
8	Abstract of 1740 Protestant householders returns	49
9	Examples of the variety in the quality of the 1766 census returns	54
10	Hearth- and poll-tax figures for Drangan parish, County Tipperary	71
11	Summary details for Crosserlough parish, County Cavan	74
12	Adjustment factors and multipliers for pre- and post-amendment hearth-rolls and for 1660 poll-tax	75
13	Adjusted population estimates for Drangan parish, County Tipperary	76
14	Entering date data in a spreadsheet	81
15	Entering monetary values in a spreadsheet	81
16	County farm totals for hearth-tax	89
17	Available hearth-money data per county	90
18	Template for recording baptisms	95

Abbreviations

Arch. Hib.	*Archivium Hibernicum*
Breifne	*Breifne. Journal of Cumann Seanchais Breifne*
Breifny	*Breifny Antiquarian Society's Journal*
D.A.	*Donegal Annual*
D.K.P.R.I.	*Report of the deputy keeper of the public records and keeper of the state papers in Ireland*
G.O.	Genealogical Office, Kildare Street, Dublin 2.
I.H.L.J.	*Irish House of Lords Journal*
I.M.C.	Irish Manuscripts Commission, 73 Merrion Square, Dublin 2. Web address: *www.irmss.ie*
J.C.D.H.S.	*Journal of the County Donegal Historical Society*
J.C.H.A.S.	*Journal of the Cork Historical & Archaeological Society*
J.C.K.A.S.	*Journal of the County Kildare Archaeological Society*
J.C.L.A.S.	*Journal of the County of Louth Archaeological Society*
J.G.A.H.S.	*The Glynns: Journal of the Glens of Antrim Historical Society*
J.R.S.A.I.	*Journal of the Royal Society of Antiquaries of Ireland*
J.W.S.E.I.A.S.	*Journal of the Waterford & South-East of Ireland Archaeological Society*
L.D.S.	Church of Jesus Christ of Latter-day Saints
N.A.I.	National Archives of Ireland, Bishop Street, Dublin 8. Web address: www.nationalarchives.ie
N.L.I.	National Library of Ireland, Kildare Street, Dublin 2. Web address: www.nli.ie
P.R.O.N.I.	Public Records Office of Northern Ireland, 66 Balmoral Avenue, Belfast, BT9 6NY. Web address: proni.nics.gov.uk
R.C.B.	Representative Church Body, Braemor Park, Rathgar, Dublin 14. Web address: ireland.anglican.org/library/library.html
R.I.A.	Royal Irish Academy, 19 Dawson Street, Dublin 2. Web address: www.ria.ie
U.C.C.	University College Cork

USEFUL LIBRARIES AND GENEALOGY SOCIETIES

British Library, 96 Euston Road, London NWI 2DB. Web address: www.bl.uk
Genealogical Society of Ireland. Web address: www.dun-laoghaire.com/genealogy
Irish Genealogical Project. Web address: www.irishgenealogy.ie
Irish public libraries, address list. Web address: www.iol.ie/~libcounc/paddress.htm
L.D.S. family search. Web address: www.familysearch.org/
Trinity College Dublin, Dublin 2. Web address: www.tcd.ie

Acknowledgements

I would like to express me thanks to the many people who assisted me during the preparation of this work. Firstly, I would like to thank Dr Mary Ann Lyons for entrusting this work to me and for providing every support and assistance requested of her. Dr Lyons' studious eye spotted many errors in my drafts for which I am most thankful and she has helped impose a structure and uniformity on the text, which would otherwise have been lacking. Also, I wish to thank Dr Raymond Gillespie who quickly responded to my many pleas for help during the project. Dr Gillespie has shown me remarkable and undeserved patience and has provided me with assistance and encouragement in abundance in the past. I would also like to thank Professor Kerby Miller who provided me with information on various pre-census sources and to Dr Marie Louise Legg for helping me with the 1749 census of Elphin. I would like to thank the Council of Trustees of the National Library of Ireland for permission to replicate a page from MS. 6054 in this book. Thanks are also due to the staff of the National Library of Ireland, the National Archives, the Representative Church Body Library (particularly Dr Susan Hood), and the Public Records Office of Northern Ireland who were all courteous and most helpful. Also, the staff of the libraries in St Patrick's College, Maynooth and U.C.D. and the staff of a great many of the public libraries throughout Ireland (particularly Michael Kelleher in Bray, County Wicklow) were most helpful in providing me with essential information.

In conclusion may I take this opportunity to thank my wife, Mary, who has supported and tolerated my studies for a number of years now and without whose encouragement I would not have been able to complete this project.

Introduction

> Place is not the crucial variable for the local historian ... It is the people
> who occupied that place, whether townland, county or diocese, which
> should be our main concern.[1]

Local history is focussed on the study of relations between people and the
various interacting social networks that governed their society. The population
of an area at a particular time, and more importantly changing population trends
over a period of time, impinged on all aspects of daily life and determined to a
great extent the relationships between the members of a local community.
Consider, for instance, the market for land. A low population and a consequent
abundance of land resulted in little competition for land and low rent prices. As
a population grew, and uncultivated land was brought under plough or hoof,
rents inevitably tended to increase. These higher rents encouraged the addition
of marginal lands at high marginal rents to the pool of cultivated land. This
process of reclaiming poorer lands as land prices (rents) increased occurred most
notably in Ireland in the decades before the Great Famine of 1845–51.

From this brief example concerning land availability it is clear that to understand
how a society evolved over time one must have an understanding of the changing
population pressures that influenced it. To illustrate the important influence that
population levels and population change had on societies one need only consider
the work of two pioneering demographic historians, Emmanuel Le Roy Ladurie
of *l'école d'Annales*, and the American Scholar, Philip Greven, whose ground-
breaking works are essential reading for those wishing to undertake serious
demographic study. Ladurie's *Les Paysans de Languedoc*, published in France
in 1966, remains an internationally recognised masterpiece of historical
investigation – a 'total history'.[2] The main theme of this book, 'the Malthusian
dilemma of a traditional agrarian society incapable, over the long run, of
preserving a balance between population and food production', bears an
obvious, if depressing, similarity to the Irish historical experience. Ladurie used
taille and *compoix* (taxation and land register) returns to study population change
in Languedoc in the three centuries following the Black Death of 1348 and the
consequent changes in society, most particularly the impact on standards of
living, which occurred as a result of those changing levels of population. He
recounts that during the course of his study, he came to realise that he was
observing 'the immense respiration of a social structure'[3] as firstly the population

1 Raymond Gillespie, 'People, place, and time' in Raymond Gillespie (ed.), *Cavan: essays
on the history of an Irish county* (Dublin, 1995), p. 11.   2 Emanuel Le Roy Ladurie, *The*

advanced and subdivision of lands commenced in the middle years of the fourteenth century and then fell back in the period 1450–1500 (consolidation of land holdings occurred) when pauperisation followed in the wake of this population increase. The population began to increase again and land subdivision recommenced at the start of the sixteenth century. This process continued until *c.*1680 when once again the population began to fall and consolidation of holdings recurred. The structuring of Ladurie's work is particularly impressive as he does not jump to conclusions based on scant evidence but tries to confirm and reconfirm trends where possible by introducing new evidence, new analyses and new approaches.

Philip Greven also used demographic analysis to study changes in society in Andover, Massachusetts, during the first hundred years or so of the colony's existence (1646–*c.*1760).[4] In the early years of the settlement the reader is introduced to a town with a low population and an abundance of land. A healthy and benign environment meant that the citizens lived long lives in comparison with their European contemporaries and a highly patriarchal society developed as a result. In the early years of the settlement the low population facilitated the first- and second-generation landowners to divide their lands among *all* of their sons after they died. By the early years of the eighteenth century, however, the population had increased substantially and land had consequently become a scarce commodity. As a result of the increased demand for land, third-generation fathers found it more difficult to provide land for all of their sons and the inheritance pattern exhibited during the first half century of the colony's existence (partible inheritance) was replaced by impartible inheritance. Under this new system the eldest son received the farm after the father's death and the remaining sons were established in a trade or encouraged to migrate to thinly populated lands beyond the settlement. The key argument that Greven makes is that even apparently diverse features such as inheritance patterns, standards of living, poverty, health, longevity and migration levels were all inherently bound up with the changes in the population level over time.

This short book aims to demonstrate the importance of considering the demographic makeup of an area when writing its history. Attention is exclusively focussed on pre-statutory-census population sources (the first statutory census was held in Ireland in 1813) and consequently readers are advised to read this guide in conjunction with a forthcoming companion volume in this series by E. Margaret Crawford.[5] The first chapter introduces the reader to a brief history of Irish demographic study and explains what constitutes a pre-census population source. In chapter two the reader is introduced to a variety of pre-census demographic sources, commencing with seventeenth-century sources

peasants of Languedoc (Illinois, 1990 repr.).   **3** Ibid., p. 4.   **4** Philip J. Greven, *Four generations: population, land and family in colonial Andover, Massachusetts* (Cornell, 1970). **5** E. Margaret Crawford, *Counting the people: a guide to the censuses of Ireland 1813 to 1911* (Maynooth Research Guides for Irish Local History, forthcoming).

such as muster rolls dating from 1630 and also the 1660 poll-tax returns. The sources are generally discussed in chronological order, but not rigidly so. It will be evident that there is a marked imbalance in the availability of sources for various parts of the country with Ulster being particularly well covered in relative terms. The final chapter outlines possibilities for demographic research and brings some commonly encountered problems to the reader's attention. Examples of recent Irish demographic analysis are also discussed.

It is hoped that this pamphlet will encourage the reader to consider the possibilities for demographic research in any area that he or she may be studying. However, one is advised to be mindful that in undertaking demographic research, particularly in the pre-census era, no matter what one estimates the population to have been at a particular time, the estimate will almost certainly be wrong.[6] One should not, however, be disheartened by this uncertainty, or view the study of an area's population trends as a Sisyphean fruitlessness, because if the subject is approached methodically and with enthusiasm, it can prove to be a most rewarding endeavour. In particular, it will be shown that it is not population *absolutes* that should be the prime focus of a population study; rather is it population *trends* and *relative* population sizes that are most important.

6 J.J. Lee, 'On the accuracy of the pre-Famine Irish censuses' in J.M. Goldstrom and L.A. Clarkson (eds), *Irish population, economy and society* (Oxford, 1981), p. 56.

CHAPTER I

Pre-census demographic analysis in Ireland

A BRIEF HISTORY OF PRE-CENSUS IRISH
POPULATION ESTIMATION

While the earliest estimate of the population of Ireland, made by Fynes Moryson, secretary to Lord Deputy Mountjoy at the beginning of the seventeenth century, suggested 'that after the [Nine Year] war closed [c.1603] … the number of souls did not exceed 700,000 in that whole Kingdom',[1] most comments on population estimation for this country typically start with the mid-seventeenth century estimates of Sir William Petty (1623–87). Petty, an English surgeon, travelled to Ireland in 1652 as physician-general of Oliver Cromwell's army. He was appointed surveyor-general, replacing the ineffectual Benjamin Worseley, and by the mid-1650s had undertaken the first cartographic survey of Ireland, known as the 'Down Survey'. In the 1670s and 1680s Petty produced a number of national population-estimates which, though probably quite inaccurate, represent the commencement of statistical demographic analysis in Ireland. He estimated the population in 1641 at 1,466,000, an arbitrary figure he derived by calculating that, as the quantities of oxen, sheep, butter and beef exported in 1664 were one-third greater than in 1641, then the 1641 population must have been one-third greater than in 1664.[2] He estimated the population in 1652 at 850,000, with '616,000 destroyed by the Rebellion', basing this figure on his more widely known estimate of 1,100,000 for 1672.[3]

By 1676 Petty estimated the population of the country at 1,200,000[4] and by 1687 he calculated a total of 1,320,000.[5] These later estimates were based on hearth-tax returns – records of a tax introduced in 1662, which required the payment of a 2s. annual tax on each hearth in a house. They were therefore likely to have been defective for two obvious reasons. Firstly, between 1665 and 1706 the hearth-tax was 'farmed' and so government officials could, at best, have only been dealing with house-number estimates rather than actual house numbers. In addition, by basing a population estimate on the total number of houses, Petty

---

1 *Irish Builder*, xxxv, no. 801 (1 May 1893), p. 108; Herbert Wood, 'Methods of registering and estimating the population of Ireland before 1864' in *Journal of the Statistical and Social Inquiry Society of Ireland*, lxxxix (1909), pp 224–5.   2 *The economic writings of Sir William Petty together with the observations upon the bills of morality*, ed. Charles Henry Hull (2 vols, Cambridge, 1899), i, pp 149–50 (hereinafter *The economic writings of Sir William Petty*). 3 Ibid., p. 141.   4 Ibid., p. 272.   5 Ibid., ii, p. 610 (1,300,000 on p. 610).

would have had to have an accurate knowledge of the 'average' number of persons per house. It seems unlikely that Petty's *estimates* of 5·5 persons per house in 1672 and 6 persons per multi-hearth and 5 persons per single-hearth house in 1687 were soundly based (he cited no authority for these figures), if only because of the different average household size figures that he used.[6] Even from a superficial viewpoint, it is clear from Petty's figures that the population-change between 1672 and 1687 was underestimated as the varying household size figures that were used to estimate the 1687 population equated to an average household size of approximately 5.08 compared to 5.5 for 1672. If Petty had maintained the 5.5 persons-per-house multiplier this would have boosted his 1687 population estimate by 130,000. More surprisingly still, however, Petty made no attempt to estimate the number of houses that were exempt from the tax by virtue of the poverty or the avoidance of the householder. L.M. Cullen has adjusted upwards Petty's 1652 estimate to 1,403,334 and the 1672 estimate to 1,693,334, based on adjustment methods used by Professor K.H. Connell.[7]

In 1695 a poll-tax requiring the payment of one shilling per person was introduced[8] and Captain John South, one of the 1,415 Protestant commissioners appointed to collect the tax, used the returns for Counties Armagh, Louth and Meath to derive a population figure for the entire country for that year.[9] His estimate of 1,034,102 persons for the entire country is far lower than any of Petty's three post-1660 estimates and grossly underestimated the population of the country at the time.[10] South also estimated the population and the number of houses and hearths in Dublin on 10 January 1696, based on the same poll-tax returns and on the hearth tax figures for that year.[11]

That South's figures significantly underestimated the population is evident from an anonymous estimate (in the Molyneux papers) dating from 1706, which reported a national population of 1,620,901, based on hearth-tax figures for that year. This estimate is important because it represents the first presentation of

---

6 Ibid., i, p. 141, ii, p. 610.   **7** L.M. Cullen, 'Population trends in seventeenth-century Ireland' in *Economic and Social Review*, vi, no. 2 (1975), pp 152, 158.   **8** George O'Brien, *The economic history of Ireland in the seventeenth century* (Dublin, 1919), pp 232–3. See Thomas Newenham, *A view of the natural, political and commercial circumstances of Ireland* (London, 1809), appendix, p. 19, for list of those legally exempted from the tax. **9** Captain South, 'An estimate of the number of people that were in Ireland, January 10th 1695' in *Philosophical Transactions of the Royal Society of London*, xxii (1700), p. 520. **10** South's figures are available in 'An account of the number of people in the County of Ardmagh, Louth, Meath and city of Dublin with an estimate of the number of people that were in the Kingdom of Ireland ye 10th January 1695/6' (T.C.D. MS. 883 (2 vols), i, p. 74), and are replicated in Newenham, *A view of the natural, political and commercial circumstances of Ireland*, appendix, p. 19.   **11** An exact accound of ye number of houses, hearths & people in Dublin in ye 10th January 1695/6 (T.C.D. MS. 883, i, p. 83). South's figures are printed in John T. Gilbert, *Calendar of ancient records of Dublin*, vi (Dublin, 1896), pp 575–81 and in part in Patrick Fagan, 'The population of Dublin in the eighteenth century ... in *Eighteenth-century Ireland*, vi (1991), p. 151.

population figures for all counties, individually.[12] Cullen has criticised it for being too low, suggesting that the county figures are deficient and that the multipliers used to convert houses to hearths are also too low.[13] The multipliers used were 5 for a single-hearth and 7 for a multi-hearth house outside of the capital and 4½ for a single-hearth and 8½ for a multi-hearth house in Dublin city, which equated to a national multiplier of 5.26 per house. This seems a reasonable figure for the average number of people per house in early eighteenth-century Ireland.

This method of converting house figures into population estimates, which was more sophisticated than much of what had gone before because it assumed a varied household size, depending on the size of the accommodation, showed a growing awareness of the complexities involved in using taxation returns to estimate population levels. Dublin was treated as a special case in the estimate because of the many large, multi-hearth houses in the city. Interestingly, although Cullen has dismissed this estimate as being too low, it is still over 50 per cent greater than South's estimate of ten years previously. The variations in housing architecture between urban and rural areas, as suggested by this manuscript, are striking. In urban areas, of the 7,505 houses recorded in Dublin city and liberties, over 88 per cent had more than one hearth. The next highest proportion of multi-hearth houses in a city was in Derry, with slightly more than 50 per cent, while Galway had the lowest proportion of multi-hearth houses, with just 23 per cent.[14] By contrast, as can be seen from the provincial figures replicated in Table 1, only about 10 per cent of rural housing was comprised of multi-hearth

Table 1. Provincial population and house estimates for 1706

	Houses			% >1 hearth	No. of people
	1 hearth	> 1 hearth	Total		
Ulster	76,728	8,379	85,107	9.8%	442,293
Leinster excl. Dublin	74,853	9,075	83,928	10.8%	437,790
Connaught	48,285	3,524	51,809	6.8%	266,093
Munster	71,962	7,813	79,775	9.8%	414,501
Country (excl. Dublin)	271,828	28,791	300,619	9.6%	1,560,677
City & liberties of Dublin	892	6,613	7,505	88.1%	60,224
Total of whole kingdom	272,720	35,404	308,124	11.5%	308,124

(Source: T.C.D. MS. 883/2, p. 330).

12 The account of ye number of houses in … the Kingdom … Estimate of the number of people and some observations (T.C.D., MS. 883, ii, p. 330).   **13** Cullen, 'Population trends in seventeenth-century Ireland', p. 150.   **14** See P.R.O.N.I., T. 1023, for Galway city hearth-money roll for 1724. This roll also indicates the religion of the listed householders.

houses, with the exception of Connaught, where less than 7 per cent of taxed houses had more than one hearth.

The next 'national' population estimate was made by Arthur Dobbs (1689–1765) for the year 1725.[15] Dobbs,[16] from Castle Dobbs in County Antrim, was solicitor-general for Ireland and was concerned with Ireland's trade and development. Between 1729 and 1731 he produced his two-volume work, *Essay on the trade and improvement of Ireland*, which contained his population estimates. In this essay he used the hearth-money returns to estimate the number of houses in each of the counties and for Dublin city in 1712, 1718, 1725 and 1726 and also estimated the number of houses in some principal towns and cities for 1725. Dobbs modified the 1725 housing total to account for 'waste' houses and estimated the national population in 1725 to be 1,669,644. He arrived at this estimate, which he considered to be 'within the Truth', by multiplying the housing estimate for that year (382,846) by 4.36, a figure representing the average number of persons per house, which he derived 'From several Returns made to me of the Number of Persons in each family, in a great many contiguous Parishes in the County of Antrim'.[17] Even Dobbs himself recognised the limitations of basing a 'national' population estimate on a figure for the number of persons-per-family derived from such a small part of the country. He was concerned that the figure of 4.36 persons-per-house probably erred on the low side, thereby causing him to underestimate the population and he noted that 'there may be more in a Family in some parts of the Kingdom than in the County [Antrim] from whence I took my Estimate'. He also noted that returns from two Dublin parishes recorded 12$\frac{1}{12}$ per house.[18] Dobbs did not actually estimate the population for 1712, 1718 and 1726. He simply recorded the housing stock figures for these years. However, corresponding population figures, based on an average household size of 6, were attributed to him in the commissioners' report for the 1821 Census.[19]

By the 1730s it was clear to government that long-standing official attempts to check the growth of Catholicism had failed. Concerned about this failure and wishing to determine the extent of the growth of 'popery', the Irish House of Lords ordered an inquiry into the state of Catholicism in Ireland in 1731, placing particular emphasis on the determination of the number of Mass houses and 'Popish schools'.[20] Returns were sought both from the administrative (the high-sheriffs of the counties and the chief magistrates of every town) and the religious (parish ministers) organs of the state so that comparisons could be made

---

15 Arthur Dobbs, *An essay on the trade and improvement of Ireland* (2 vols, Dublin, 1729–31), ii, p. 9.   16 Leslie Stephen and Sidney Lee (eds), *The dictionary of national biography*, v (London, 1973 repr.), pp 1035–7. 17 Dobbs, *Trade*, p. 9.   18 Ibid., pp 9–10.   19 *Abstract of the answers and returns pursuant to act 55 Geo. 3, for taking account of the population of Ireland in 1821*, H.C. 1824 (577), xxii, 411, p. vii.   20 Committee appointed on 2 November 1731 (*I.H.L.J.*, iii (1727–52), p. 159) and resolved, 10 November, that heads of bills to disarm papists be prepared (*I.H.L.J.*, iii, pp 161–2).

between data collected by the two sources. The returns for Galway and Mayo were read to the House on 6 December 1731[21] and a general report for the country was read on 8 March 1732.[22] The detailed returns for the entire country were published in various volumes of *Analecta Hibernica* in the 1910s.[23]

Contemporaneous with this inquiry, a religious census was to be carried out by the clergy of the Church of Ireland and the magistracy. As early as 1821 the deficiencies in this census were recognised when in the preliminary observations on the 1821 census it was noted that

> On reflecting on the state of Ireland at that period, when large tracts of the country were not subject to the jurisdiction of the former of those classes [magistracy], or to the influence of the latter [Church of Ireland clergy], the result of an inquiry made by either of them, when unsupported by the authority of an Act of Legislature, must be deemed far from satisfactory.[24]

Despite this weakness, the estimate is of particular importance for two reasons. Firstly, as the returns were made by the Church of Ireland clergy and by magistrates in towns and cities and by high sheriffs in the counties, this is the only eighteenth-century 'national' population estimate not based on housing aggregates from hearth-tax returns. This gives the demographic historian a useful alternative with which the various hearth-tax-based figures may be compared. Secondly, this is the first eighteenth-century return that estimated formally the religious breakdown of the citizens of the island. Nationally, the population was estimated at 2,010,219, with Protestants reputedly outnumbering Catholics in only one of the four provinces, Ulster. The returns are shown in Table 2 below.

Table 2. Religious breakdown estimates for 1731

	Prots.	RCs	Total	% Prot	% RC
Ulster	360,630	158,028	518,658	69.53%	30.47%
Leinster	203,087	447,916	651,003	31.20%	68.80%
Munster	115,130	482,044	597,174	19.28%	80.72%
Connaught	21,604	221,780	243,384	8.88%	91.12%
Total	700,451	1,309,768	**2,010,219**	34.84%	65.16%

(Source: Thomas Newenham, *A view of the natural, political and commercial circumstances of Ireland*, appendix, p. 19).

21 *I.H.L.J.*, iii, pp 168–72.   **22** *I.H.L.J.*, iii, pp 199–202, 207–10.   **23** 'Report on the state of Popery, Ireland, 1731 (Ulster)' in *Arch. Hib.*, i (1912), pp 10–27 for Ulster; 'Report on the state of Popery in Ireland, 1731 Munster' in *Arch. Hib.*, ii (1913), pp 108–56 for Munster; 'Report on the state of Popery in Ireland, 1731' in *Arch. Hib.*, iii (1914), pp 124–59 for Connaught; 'Report on the state of Popery in Ireland, 1731' in *Arch. Hib.*, iv (1915), pp 131–77 for Leinster.   **24** *Abstract of the answers and returns ... of the population*

The following year another religious census was conducted but in this case the estimates were based on the housing figures returned by the hearth-money collectors who were instructed to determine the religious breakdown of the people in the area for which they were responsible.[25] The estimate, published anonymously but almost certainly the work of David Bindon,[26] a member of the Irish House of Commons, estimated that there was 386,902 families in the country exclusive of soldiers and their families, residents of colleges, hospitals and poor-houses and the more than '2000 Certificate-Houses (as those are called which by reason of their Poverty are excused from paying Hearthmoney)'.[27] If these exempt groups were included, the author suggested that these housing figures translate into a population estimate of 'very near Two Millions of Inhabitants'.[28]

Table 3. Housing-stock estimates for 1732. The population estimates excluding soldiers, hospital residents etc. were not reported in the article but calculated using a multiplier of 5.

	Houses estimate					Population estimate		
	Prots.	RCs	Total	% Prot	% RC	Prots.	RCs	Total
Ulster	62,624	38,459	101,083	61.95%	38.05%	313,120	192,295	505,415
Leinster	25,241	92,434	117,675	21.45%	78.55%	126,205	462,170	588,375
Munster	13,337	106,407	119,744	11.14%	88.86%	66,685	532,035	598,720
Connaught	4,299	44,101	48,400	8.88%	91.12%	21,495	220,505	242,000
Total	105,501	281,401	**386,902**	27.27%	72.73%	527,505	1,407,005	**1,934,510**

(Source: [David Bindon?], *An abstract of the number of Protestant and Popish families in the several counties and provinces of Ireland*, p. 6.).

While this 1732 estimate only contains provincial housing-stock numbers, if provincial populations are estimated by applying an average household size of 5 to the figures, as Bindon had done for the national household total,[29] then the population figures can be compared with the 1731 census figures. In Table 4 the total numbers of Protestants and Catholics as reported by the 1731 and 1732 'censuses' are distributed among the provinces and, as can be seen, the results for 1732 are quite different from those reported by the 1731 census. The 1731

of Ireland in 1821, p. vi.   **25** [David Bindon ?], *An abstract of the number of Protestant and Popish families in the several counties and provinces of Ireland, taken from the returns made by the hearthmoney collectors to the hearthmoney office in Dublin in the years 1732 and 1733* (Dublin, 1736).   **26** Gerard McCoy, '"Patriots, Protestants and Papists": religion and the ascendancy, 1714–60' in *Bullán: an Irish Studies Journal*, i, no. 1 (1994), p. 106.   **27** [Bindon?], *An abstract of the number of Protestant and Popish families in the several counties and provinces of Ireland*, p. 7.   **28** Ibid., p. 9.   **29** Ibid., p. 8.

estimate, for instance, reported that 51 per cent of all Protestants in Ireland were living in Ulster whereas the 1732 estimate suggested that over 59 per cent of Protestants lived in that province.

Table 4. Distribution of Protestants and Catholics between provinces as reported by the 1731 and 1732 'censuses'

% of total	1731			1732 excluding noted exemptions		
	Prots.	RCs	Total	Prots.	RCs	Total
Ulster	51.49%	12.07%	25.80%	59.36%	13.67%	26.13%
Leinster	28.99%	34.20%	32.38%	23.92%	32.85%	30.41%
Munster	16.44%	36.80%	29.71%	12.64%	37.81%	30.95%
Connaught	3.08%	16.93%	12.11%	4.07%	15.67%	12.51%

Unquestionably, the 1732 estimate is defective. Connell revised the figures upwards by over 50 per cent to 3,018,000 and more recently Dickson *et al.* have estimated the 1732 population at between 2,160,000 and 2,530,000.[30] The real importance of this estimate, however, lies in the fact that for the first time, barony population figures were recorded from the hearth-tax data. However, these barony figures, available on microfilm in the P.R.O.N.I.,[31] should be used with extreme caution, as it is clear that they were not meticulously recorded, with figures for some baronies missing and, in many cases, baronies are included in the wrong counties.

From the 1730s, the number of houses per county, as returned by the hearth-money collectors, was published annually in *Watson's Triple Almanac*. Although the earliest listings can be ignored as they merely repeat housing totals that are available in some of the sources mentioned above, unique housing totals are listed in various editions of the almanac for 1744, 1749, 1752, 1753 and 1760.[32] The next contemporary population estimates, however, were for 1754 and 1767, both of these being based on hearth-tax housing returns. In 1754 the housing stock was recorded at 395,439, rising to 424,646 by 1767 and a persons-per-house multiplier of 6 was used to translate these housing estimates into population figures of 2,372,634 and 2,544,276 respectively.[33] Later, Richard Price applied a multiplier of 4.5 to the 1767

30 K.H. Connell, *The population of Ireland, 1750–1845* (Oxford, 1950), p. 25; David Dickson, Cormac Ó Gráda and Stuart Daultrey, 'Hearth tax, household size and Irish population change 1672–1821' in *Proceedings of the Royal Irish Academy*, lxxxii, C, no. 6 (1982), p. 156. 31 An abstract of the number of Protestant and Popish families as returned to the Hearth money office Anno 1732 pursuant to the order of the commissioner of revenue (Lambeth Palace Library, MS. 1742, ff 43–8 [P.R.O.N.I., Microfilm 310]). 32 *Watson's Triple Almanac* (1748), p. 26 for 1744; ibid. (1751), p. 28 for 1749; ibid. (1753), p. 28 for 1752; ibid. (1757), p. 31 for 1753; ibid. (1763), p. 30, for 1760.   33 Thomas Newenham, *A statistical and historical inquiry into the progress and magnitude of the population of Ireland* (London, 1805), p. 94.

housing figures to estimate the population at slightly more than 1.9 millions. In like fashion, a multiplier of 6 was used to estimate the population at 2,690,556 from the 1777 hearth-tax returns whereas James Laffan used a multiplier of 5.5 to produce a figure which was about 9 per cent less.[34]

In the meantime, within three decades of initiating the 1730s population inquiry, the Irish House of Lords had instigated at least two further inquiries into Irish population in order to determine the country's religious makeup. The first attempt, in 1764, failed and so the Lords ordered the parish incumbents to return to them complete lists of Protestant and Papist householders within their parishes in March and April 1766. The extant returns from this census are patchy and range from little or nothing for many parts of the country to some very diligently transcribed and detailed parish lists for other parts. However, no 'national' population estimate was ever reported from this census as some parishes failed to make returns.

In the latter quarter of the eighteenth century the Irish population level became a focus of debate among contemporary British social scientists, Irish social inquiry being less well developed at that time. The interest that British contemporaries took in Ireland's population history was primarily an offshoot from a preoccupation with the ongoing 'population controversy' that had started in Britain in the 1750s. British social commentators such as the Revd John Howlett and Richard Price studied Irish population figures in order to support their arguments regarding British population trends.[35] Price, a non-conformist minister, argued that England's population was falling as a result of land enclosure and Howlett, anxious to disprove this assertion, hoped to find a rapid rate of population growth in Ireland. Using hearth-tax returns, Howlett argued that 'the population of the kingdom, have [*sic*] been constantly increasing during the last hundred years' and that it 'must violate every rule of analogy to suppose that *England*, which is so closely connected with her ... should not also, in every one of these particulars, have made, in some degree, a similar advance'.[36] He believed there to be over 500,000 houses in the country in 1781, which, he suggested, indicated a population of between 2,500,000 and 2,750,000. At the same time the disputatious Richard Twiss, an English traveller who penned an unflattering portrait of Ireland following a tour of the country, assumed the average Irish household size to be 8, and estimated the 1775 population at 3,392,000.[37]

34 Ibid.; James Laffan, *Political arithmetic of the population, commerce and manufactures of Ireland* ... (Dublin, 1785), p. 1. **35** For an introduction to the population controversy in Britain see D.V. Glass, 'The population controversy in eighteenth-century England' in idem, *Numbering the people. The eighteenth-century population controversy and the development of census and vital statistics in Britain* (Farnborough, 1973), pp 11–26. **36** J. Howlett, *An essay on the population of Ireland* (London, 1786), pp 19, 24. **37** Ibid., pp 15, 17n. Richard Twiss, *A tour in Ireland in 1775* (Dublin, 1776), p. 57.

As has been seen, the accuracy of most of the eighteenth-century population estimates relied upon having accurate housing figures, derived from the hearth-tax returns, as a starting point. Two important factors, however, made it likely that the housing numbers produced by the hearth returns were deficient. Firstly, the hearth-tax was a much hated and highly regressive levy, which people went to great lengths to avoid paying. Secondly, fraud on the part of the hearth-tax collectors was rife and seems to have been a growing problem as the eighteenth century progressed. For these reasons it appears likely that the *discrepancy* between the hearth-tax housing-stock figures and the *actual* number of houses was increasing as time went on. It was primarily because of the obvious fraud being perpetrated by hearth-tax collectors that the administration of the hearth-tax was overhauled in the 1780s, under the management of Gervais Parker Bushe, a Revenue Board commissioner. The results of Bushe's endeavours are readily apparent from the number of houses returned by the collectors, which increased by 31 per cent in the three years from 1785 (474,237 houses) to 1788 (621,484 houses).[38] Despite this increase Bushe believed the actual number of houses in the country in 1788 to be more likely 650,000 or as high as 680,000 and he estimated the population at above 4,040,000.[39] By contrast, an estimate for 1787, based on the pre-Bushe hearth-tax figures, reckoned that the population to be 'above 3,000,000'.[40] The writer and one time MP for Clonmel, Thomas Newenham (1762–1831), accepted Bushe's augmented figures and, using a multiplier of 6, estimated the 1788 population at 3,900,000.[41]

By the late eighteenth century it was evident to observers that the population of the country was increasing at an unprecedented rate.[42] The celebrated English traveller and agricultural commentator, Arthur Young (1741–1820), for instance, regularly remarked on the rapid increase in population in various districts as he travelled about the country, and urged the Irish legislature 'to order an actual enumeration of the whole people'.[43] However, it was to be a further four decades before a census was carried out. Young did not try to compute the population of the country but concluded that the hearth-money returns of £61,646 suggested a population of at least three millions.[44]

The hearth-tax, the basis for most seventeenth- and eighteenth-century population estimates was introduced more or less contemporaneously in Ireland and

38 *Journal of the House of Commons of Ireland*, xii, App. P. cclvi for 1785 and Newenham, *Population of Ireland*, p. 72 for 1788.   **39** Gervais Parker Bushe, 'An essay towards ascertaining the population of Ireland' in *Transactions of the Royal Irish Academy*, iii (1790), pp 146–7.   **40** *The compleat Irish traveller containing a general description of the most noted cities, towns, seats buildings, loughs &c in the kingdom of Ireland* (2 vols, London, 1788), i, p. xxv.   **41** Newenham, *Population of Ireland*, p. 94.   **42** For examples see Arthur Young, *A tour in Ireland . . . in the years 1776, 1777 and 1778* (Dublin, 1780), i, pp 127–8, 129 where he states that the population around Newtown Mount Kennedy was increasing rapidly. Also see J. Howlett, 'An essay on the population of Ireland' in J.J. Lee (ed.), *The population of Ireland before the nineteenth century* (1973), pp 16–24.   **43** Young, *A tour in Ireland* (Dublin, 1780), ii, p. 88.   **44** Ibid., p. 199.

England. It was abandoned in England in 1689 but remained on the statute books in Ireland until 1824.[45] This tax placed a heavy burden on the poor in particular. It was noted in 1792, for instance, that 'In years of plenty and cheapness, with an industrious family and sobriety this [cottier] class may be able to pay the [hearth] tax; but in case of the reverse, or any material misfortune, the tax might be distressing'.[46] The tax was reformed in 1793 when most houses with one hearth or less were exempted from the tax,[47] a sweeping reform that exempted the vast bulk of former taxpayers and meant that the hearth-tax was no longer a suitable instrument for approximating the size of the housing stock. The last pre-reform hearth figures available, therefore, are for 1791. From these a national population of 4,206,612 was estimated, based on the assumption that the average household size was six.[48] The Revd Daniel Beaufort (1739–1821), vicar of the Navan union of parishes in County Meath and author of *Memoir of a map of Ireland*, also used the 1791 figures to estimate a national population of 3,850,000 by using a multiplier of 5.5.[49]

Despite the contemporary interest in the rate of population increase, Ireland was excluded from the first British census in 1801.[50] A bill for the holding of a belated Irish census was introduced in the House of Commons in 1806 but failed and Ireland was again excluded from the second British census in 1811. The following year, however, another bill for holding an Irish census became law and the first official census of the nineteenth century commenced in Ireland on 1 May 1813.[51] However, as this census had not been completed by March 1815, the enumeration was abandoned.[52] The next census in 1821 was kingdom-wide and was completed successfully in Ireland although its accuracy is to be doubted. Censuses were subsequently held every ten years in Ireland from 1821 until the last all-Ireland census was held in 1911.

PRE-CENSUS SUBSTITUTES

As regular censuses were not introduced in Ireland until the second decade of the nineteenth century local historians must look to alternative population sources to determine population levels in an area for the pre-census period. Unsurprisingly, however, suitable population sources are a rarity. For a source to be a suitable vehicle for determining the population of an area at a particular time it must fulfil a number of criteria. Firstly, the source has to have been *near-universal*; that is to say the source must be a record of an enumeration of the vast

45 Stuart Daultrey, David Dickson and Cormac Ó Grada, 'Eighteenth-century Irish population: new perspectives from old sources' in *Journal of Economic History*, xli, no. 3 (1981), p. 603. **46** L.M. Cullen, *An economic history of Ireland since 1660* (London, 1987), pp 70–1. **47** 'Hearth money rolls of County Louth' ed. Charles McNeill in *J.C.L.A.S.* (1925), vi, no. 1, p. 82. **48** Connell, *Population*, p. 4. **49** Ibid., p. 4n. **50** D.V. Glass and P.A.M. Taylor, *Population and emigration* (Dublin, 1976), p. 11. **51** Ibid. **52** Ibid.

majority of people in a community or groups within a community. Typical near-universal sources include records of taxes payable by the entire community, such as the hearth-tax, but may also include records like muster rolls (records of persons available for military service) which were usually limited to the Church of Ireland community. Secondly, the reason for compiling the source must be known. This is a very important factor as knowledge of the reasoning behind the recording of the data helps the historian make a judgement as to the reliability of the source. If groups of people were intentionally omitted from the source, it must be possible to make a considered estimate as to the extent of the omissions from the source and this cannot be done accurately without knowing the origin of the source.

Furthermore, it is useful to know who actually compiled the source as this can also give some guidance as to the completeness of the data. For instance, if a Church of Ireland minister compiled a listing of his parishioners, it is reasonable to presume that the degree of completeness of the listing would have been influenced by factors such as the religious balance in his community, the size of the parish, the length of time he was stationed in the parish and the interest he took in the day-to-day running of parish business. If a minister was an absentee he could not be expected to have had as intimate a knowledge of his incumbency as would a minister who was resident in a small, compact parish. Thirdly, the spatial extent of the returns must be known as sources of different origin recorded varied data according to a multiplicity of rules. A religious census, for instance, had a different focus to that of a taxation return and it is highly probable that the boundaries of parishes reported in a religious census may not have coincided with the boundaries used in contemporary taxation returns. This is all the more likely because many parishes had very small Protestant congregations and ministers were, therefore, frequently responsible for a number of contiguous parishes, known as *unions*. Often if a parish minister was making a religious census return he would report figures for his 'union' whereas taxation figures would usually have been compiled on a parish basis. To further complicate the matter, the boundaries of parishes and townlands were often mutable before they were strictly plotted by the Ordnance Survey in the early nineteenth century.

Considering the above requirements, pre-census sources that have merit for demographic research fall broadly into five categories, these being universal taxation returns, returns listing availability for military service, religious censuses, church records and estate records. In the following chapters these sources will be examined in detail and specifically the potential of each type of source for demographic analysis will be considered.

CHAPTER 2

Sources for pre-census population studies

This chapter aims to detail the principal demographic sources available to the local historian and to suggest how the researcher might go about locating and using those sources. Unfortunately the vast majority of the sources in question were stored in the Public Records Office, based in the Four Courts in Dublin, during the Irish Civil War and were destroyed in an explosion in June 1922. Without doubt the destruction of the P.R.O. and the consequent loss of much of Ireland's administrative heritage has seriously hampered demographic study in this country, although the loss has not proved as great as it might have been because some sources had been copied prior to the explosion. However, any researcher wishing to undertake a demographic study of an area should prepare himself or herself for the disappointment of discovering that some of the sources hereinafter described simply will not exist for the area in which he or she is interested. Although an attempt has been made to cover as wide a range of sources as possible, in only a few cases will researchers have all of these sources available for the area that they are studying.

There are a number of important repositories for pre-census primary source material in Ireland and abroad. Principal among these are, in Dublin, the National Library of Ireland in Kildare Street, the National Archives of Ireland in Bishop Street and the Representative Church Body Library in Braemor Park, Churchtown and, in Belfast, the Public Records Office of Northern Ireland, on Balmoral Avenue. Many county libraries have also endeavoured to obtain copies of pre-census population data for their local history collections. In addition, some local history societies have published various demographic source materials in their associated journals over the years, thus making the sources available to a wider audience.

CURRENT THOUGHTS ON IRISH DEMOGRAPHY

A notable feature of the pre-census 'national' population estimates alluded to in the first chapter is that many of those involved in calculating the various estimates aimed to produce a specific population figure by simply applying a multiplier, representing the average number of persons per house, to the housing-stock figure. In many cases little or no effort was made to determine the degree of omission from the hearth-tax returns, even though it would have been quite apparent to the authors that the returns were deficient. It will be seen later, for instance, that William Hardinge, using a national poll-tax summary for 1660 (which he believed to be a census for 1659), estimated the population of Ireland at 500,091,[1] this figure having been reached by aggregating the available figures and adding in estimates for areas for which no data survived. Even William Shaw Mason, 'the father of the Irish census', recounted that Patrick Lynch, an 'ingenious friend', had calculated the population of Ireland in 1813 to be 'nearly 5,957,856'.[2] Nowadays it is understood that producing exact figures like these is quite meaningless as estimates generated from taxation returns or determined by deriving estimates for missing figures are inherently error prone. If Hardinge, for instance, was publishing his estimate today he would report the population to have been 'approximately 500,000' rather than 500,091.

Indeed, all of the eighteenth-century estimates are based on figures that were accumulated over a period of time rather than on a particular day. Even the earliest Irish censuses were not held on a specific day but were rather *viva-voce* enquiries that continued over a period of months.[3] This was another fact that was simply ignored by the contributors to the population debates, with little attention being afforded the question of the day or period of time referred to in the estimate. Although the participants in the 'population debate' were keenly aware of this limitation with respect to the hearth-tax and other sources, most chose to gloss over this fact and focussed on produced specific, if meaningless, population estimates.

Modern historians recognise that specific population figures for the pre-census period cannot be produced from the sketchy evidence that is available to us and are more clearly aware of the deficiencies that may exist in the various sources and of how one should take account of missing data. Furthermore, demographers today tend to refer to estimates as being 'in the order of' a particular number, and generally round up or down to the nearest hundred or thousand any calculated estimate. It is important that this trend be continued in future demographic research. In fact, one will probably find that focussing on absolute figures is more of a distraction than a benefit as the actual population of an area at a particular time is really quite incidental. William Smyth (Professor of geography, U.C.C.), for instance, in discussing the 1660 poll-tax returns, advises that rather than working with absolute figures, the historian's emphasis should be on inter-baronial comparisons.[4] So too on a smaller scale, in the

1 W. H. Hardinge, 'Observations on the earliest known manuscript census returns of the people of Ireland' in *Transactions of the Royal Irish Academy, xxiv*, no. 2 (1867), p. 326. **2** William Shaw Mason, *A statistical account or parochial survey of Ireland* (3 vols, Dublin, 1814–19), iii, pp xxi n, xlviii. **3** The first Irish 'census day' was 6 June 1841, this being the fourth attempt at a statutory national enumeration. J.J. Lee, 'On the accuracy of pre-Famine Irish censuses', p. 53. **4** William J. Smyth, 'Society and settlement in seventeenth-century Ireland: the evidence of the '1659 Census" in William J. Smyth and

majority of cases one will derive more benefit from analysing the *relative* sizes of populations in neighbouring areas and accounting for changes in these *relative* sizes over time, than from estimating *absolute* numbers.

That one particular area was populated more or less quickly than a neighbouring area is a curiosity that the local historian should endeavour to explain. Indeed, one should try to avoid studying a specific area as it is of greater historical interest to account for the varying trends *between* areas rather than simply looking at a *single* area in isolation. Readers are therefore advised to avoid concentrating their energies primarily on the derivation of absolute population figures and are instead urged to expand their research to cover areas outside of the region with which they are principally concerned as this will aid the construction of a more complete population picture for their area of interest.

CENSUS SUBSTITUTES

As censuses *per se* did not commence in Ireland until the early years of the nineteenth century, historians must look to other sources for data intimating population levels or population trends. In the first chapter it was noted that for sources to be useful in building up a picture of population levels and changing population trends in the community as a whole, they must be comprehensive, accurate and representative of the entire population or of an identifiable community. The first port of call for a researcher looking for suitable sources is the indispensable *Manuscript sources for the history of Irish civilisation* edited by Richard Hayes.[5] Its eleven volumes (plus three supplementary volumes) provide a reasonably comprehensive, if somewhat dated, listing of the sources deposited in the National Library of Ireland, the National Archives, the P.R.O.N.I. and in various other repositories in Ireland and abroad. Volumes 5 and 6 present a grouping of sources by 'subject' (population, censuses and hearth money, for instance) thereby enabling the researcher to quickly locate appropriate source material. Volumes 7 and 8 group the sources by county under the four sub-headings, 'General and miscellaneous', 'Estates', 'Maps' and 'Places'.

Hayes' catalogue is very easy to use but does contain mistakes and omissions. Thus, it is good practice when looking for pre-census population sources to consult the *Subjects* volumes, under population, taxation, hearth-money and so on, and the *Places* volumes under the area being studied, as sources are occasionally omitted from one or other of the volumes. It is important to use the three supplement volumes also as these contain various sources omitted from the original catalogue. In addition, Hayes edited a nine-volume set of listings of

Kevin Whelan (eds), *Common ground: essays on the historical geography of Ireland* (Cork, 1988), p. 56.   **5** Richard Hayes, *Manuscript sources for the history of Irish civilisation* (11 vols, Boston, 1965); idem, *Manuscript sources for the history of Irish civilisation: first supplement* (3

articles that appeared in Irish periodicals (*Sources for the history of Irish civilisation: articles in Irish periodicals*) and these should also be referenced as much pre-census population source-material (some now lost) has been published in various journals and periodicals.[6]

A typical entry in *Manuscript sources for the history of Irish civilisation* lists the location and identification number of the original source material, briefly describes the contents of the source and notes the microfilm numbers if the source was available on microfilm in the National Library when Hayes compiled the catalogue. The following entry in *Manuscript sources*, vi (the second *Subjects* volume), under the heading 'Population' is typical:[7]

Population:
London: British Museum: Add. Ms. 18,022: (Extract). An exact account of the number of houses, hearths and people (totalled for each parish) in Dublin, Jan. 10, 1695 (1696).

                     n. 780   p. 506

The entry thus provides sufficient details to enable the researcher to locate the source. The original of this source is located in the British Library (which was formed from the British Museum in 1973) in London and can be obtained by requesting Add. MS. (additional manuscript) 18,022. Although it is not explicitly specified, the source is a poll-tax and hearth-tax abstract that was compiled by Captain John South from returns that were recorded on 10 January 1696 (new date). The *n.* and *p.* numbers at the end of the reference are National Library microfilm numbers. When an entry contains microfilm numbers it means that a microfilm copy of the source is available in the National Library in Dublin and can be viewed by requesting the *p.* number (which refers to the positive microfilm) for the film.

Genealogy books are also worth referencing when undertaking a demographic study. The two publications most widely used today are John Grenham's *Tracing your Irish ancestors* and the superior James G. Ryan's *Irish records: sources for family and local history*.[8] Both works contain a chapter listing a variety of genealogical sources – published and manuscript – for each county and copies of either or both of the books are available in most public libraries. For Northern Ireland, Ian Maxwell's *Tracing your ancestors in Northern Ireland*, published in 1997, should also be consulted.[9] Donal Begley's *Irish genealogy: a record finder* was popular when

vols, Boston, 1979).   **6** Idem, *Sources for the history of Irish civilisation: articles in Irish periodicals* (9 vols, Boston, 1970).   **7** Hayes, *Manuscript sources*, vi, p. 324. For a consideration of this particular source see Fagan, 'The population of Dublin in the eighteenth century', pp 125-8.   **8** John Grenham, *Tracing your Irish ancestors: the complete guide* (Dublin, 1992); James G. Ryan, *Irish records: sources for family and local history* (Salt Lake City, 1997).   **9** Ian Maxwell, *Tracing your ancestors in Northern Ireland: a guide to ancestry*

it was published in the early 1980s but is less widely used today.[10] With the increase in popularity of genealogy, books on the subject focussing on individual counties have begun to appear in recent years. Flyleaf Press has lately produced genealogy pamphlets for Counties Cork, Donegal, Dublin, Mayo and Kerry, of which the Dublin and Cork pamphlets are most useful and the Ulster Historical Foundation has published reference texts for Counties Armagh and Down, the first of a planned six county guides for Northern Ireland.[11]

It should be remembered, of course, that genealogy books are necessarily geared towards providing the reader with a guide to genealogical sources – essentially lists of names. In many cases the sources referenced in genealogy books are of little use to the demographic historian as there may be no indication as to why the list was compiled or how comprehensive it was. Nonetheless, it is always worth referencing these books to ascertain if they list sources that may prove useful for local demographic research.

Local histories and local journals can also be excellent sources of demographic data as many local journals have transcribed some of the more important census substitutes for their particular area. Hearth-money rolls, the 1766 religious census and private local censuses have been particularly popular targets for enthusiastic local historians, antiquarian scholars and copyists. The older local history journals such as the *Journal of the Cork Historical & Archaeological Society*, the *Journal of the County of Louth Archaeological Society*, the *Clogher Record* or *Seanchas Ardmhacha* have been to the forefront in publishing census-substitute data but even some of the newer journals have reproduced census-substitute transcriptions that are invaluable to any researcher undertaking a demographic study.[12]

Similarly, local histories, particularly those written before or shortly after the destruction of the P.R.O., should also be consulted as they can contain census-substitute transcriptions. Particular attention should be paid to parochial histories as their authors, many of whom were clerics, often reproduced data from various religious censuses. The parochial succession lists and local history writings of the Revd Michael Comerford and the indefatigable Canon James B. Leslie in particular feature transcriptions, records of religious censuses and hearth-roll aggregates that were lost in 1922.[13] Researchers using Leslie's succession lists are

research in the Public Records Office of Northern Ireland (Belfast, 1997).   **10** Donal F. Begley (ed.), *Irish genealogy: a record finder* (Dublin, 1981).   **11** James G. Ryan and Brian Smith, *Tracing your Dublin ancestors* (Dublin, 1988); Tony McCarthy and Tim Cadogan, *Tracing your Cork ancestors* (Dublin, 1998); Ian Maxwell, *Researching Armagh ancestors: a practical guide for the family and local historian* (Belfast, 2000); idem, *Researching Down ancestors: a practical guide for the family and local historian* (Belfast, 2001).   **12** *Journal of the South Derry Historical Society*, for instance, has carried 1766 religious census transcriptions, edited by Diarmaid Ó Doibhlin, for various south Derry parishes in its earlier issues.   **13** M. Comerford, *Collections relating to the dioceses of Kildare and Leighlin* (3 vols, Dublin, 1883), i, pp 261–74; iii, pp 404–7; James B. Leslie, *Clogher clergy and parishes* (Enniskillen, 1929),

advised that population figures, if recorded, are usually listed in the parish notes at the end of each parish listing (see bibliography for a list of his principal publications).

Although publication of sources in local journals and local histories intro-duces census substitutes to a wider audience by making it easier for people to access the data, the researcher should always endeavour to consult the original source rather than relying solely on a transcription, if at all possible. Transcribing lists of names is a tedious task and even the most committed copyist can easily make mistakes. In addition, the original sources may be damaged or written in scarcely-legible script and consequently the published work will only represent the reader's *interpretation* of what is written in the source. If one chooses to use a transcription, therefore, one's research is dependent on the accuracy of the copyist and the integrity of the printing process and will be compromised by any mistakes made in replicating the data. While the originals of many population sources have been destroyed in 1922, researchers ought to seek to consult the earliest possible transcription and preferably one that was directly transcribed from the original.

For example, consider the 1665 hearth-tax roll for Fahan parish, County Donegal, which was published in an early volume of the *Donegal Annual*.[14] This was copied from a transcription located in the Public Records Office in Belfast. In the P.R.O.N.I. transcription, at the end of the listing of parish householders, it is stated that there were 110 households in the roll and this statement is faithfully reproduced in the *Donegal Annual* copy. However, a count of the names on the roll in the P.R.O.N.I. copy confirms that there were 110 tax-paying householders in 1665. Eight householders were therefore inadvertently omitted from the *Donegal annual* transcription which contains only 102 householders – a salutory warning regarding the perils of research based on the published rather than the original source.

PRE–CENSUS POPULATION SOURCES –
POLL–TAX SUMMARY, 1660

As already illustrated in the previous chapter, returns from near-universal taxations are an important pre-census population source for the Irish local historian. A convenient starting point for seventeenth-century population studies, therefore, is the 1660 poll-tax summary, often inaccurately referred to as 'the 1659 census' or 'Pender's census'.[15] This summary was compiled by Sir William Petty from the returns of the poll-tax collectors, presumably as an aid

pp 261–2.   **14** *Donegal Annual*, v, no. 1 (1961), pp 88–9.   **15** *A census of Ireland circa 1659, with supplementary material from the poll money ordinances, 1660–1661*, ed. Seamus Pender (Dublin, 1939) (hereinafter *Census Ire., 1659*).

Figure 1. Sample page from 1660 poll-tax summary

308 CENSUS OF IRELAND, 1659

Parishes	Places	Numbs of People	Tituladoes Names	English	Irish
Colloman P'ish	Rathdron	14			14
	Josinstowne	21			21
	Kylerke	33			33
	Mocklerstowne	40		2	38
Morestowne Kirke P'ish	Ballin Attin	52			52
	Grage ne Brenagh	3			3
	Morestowne Kirke	33			33
	Ouskeigh	10		3	7
	Pt Ballinecre	9			9
Dangonergan Parish	Shanballyduff	15			15
	Ballytarsny McCarris	22		2	20
Outragh P'ish	Outragh	62			62
Boyton ragh Parish	Boytonragh	64			64
	Templenoe	14			14
	Boystowne	23			23
(*folio* 31). Tullachmaine	Tullachmaine	42			42
	Rath McCarty	111			111
	Rathsallagh	28			28
Drangane P'ish	Drangane	10			10
	Corbally	4			4
	Ballynenane	9			9
	Newtowne	7			7
The additionalls of ol upon the revieu	[*sic* /] Midlethird				
Mogowry P'ish	Mogowry towne	5			5
Sullagh P'ish	Ballylosgy	2			2
	Lismortagh	2			2
	Killbrydy	2			2
Rathcoole P'ish	Saucestowne	4			4
	Colemoore	1			1
	Slaynestowne	5			5
	Killknockane	4			4
	Darrylusgane	4			4
Peppertowne P'ish	Rathkeny	2			2
Cromps P'ish	Crumps castle	3			3
Cloneene P'ish	Ballynard	1			1
	Milestowne	2			2
	Gortnapissy	5			5
Red City P'ish	Red City	4			4
	Barretstowne	2			2
(*folio* 32) Kiltenane Parrish	Clare	4			4
	Killoshe	14		2	12
	Behalte Collope	4			4
	Killtenane	7		1	6
	Grangbegg	4			4
St John Baptist Grange P'ish	Dromdyle	3			3
	Foulkstowne	3			3

(Source: *Census Ire., 1659*, p. 308).

to his demographic research, but was lost for generations until it was rediscovered by William Hardinge amongst the marquess of Lansdowne's papers in Lansdowne House in London in 1864.[16] Hardinge, believing that he had found 'the earliest known manuscript census returns of the people of Ireland', duly transported the returns to Dublin where they were copied. The copies were subsequently deposited in the library of the Royal Irish Academy where they have remained to this day,[17] and the originals were returned to London. Hardinge dated the manuscript data to 1659 and presented a paper on the subject of the 'census' to the Academy in 1865.[18] Allowing for the deficiencies in the figures, which are outlined below, he calculated the population in 1659 at 500,091, substantially less than Petty's 1672 estimate of 1,100,000.[19]

For the local historian these returns represent an extremely important reference point for population studies as they cover almost all of the country and present figures for areas as small as townlands or local equivalents such as ballieboes or quarters. As can be seen from the sample page from the taxation return (Figure 1), the returns are presented for each barony in columnar fashion (no baronial divisions given for Counties Fermanagh and Monaghan), as follows:

Table 5. Typical structure of data presented in the 1660 poll-tax return

Parishes	Generally lists the name of a parish but may also list towns or other macro-divisions. In some instances the parish names are omitted – e.g. barony of Rathdown in Dublin.
Townlands	Lists the names of townlands or alternative micro-divisions in the parishes listed in the first column.
Number of people	A number beside each of the named townlands shows the number of poll-tax payers. Hardinge incorrectly believed this figure to be the number of people inhabiting the townland.
Tituladoes' names[20]	Records names of persons under various townlands. Usually these persons are recorded as 'gent'[lemen] or 'Esq'[uires] and so on. In towns the titulado's occupation is often listed. Simington describes tituladoes as 'persons holding title of honour'.[21]
English (& Scottish)	The number of English taxpayers in each townland. In some cases, principally in Ulster, the number includes Scottish taxpayers.
Irish	The number of Irish taxpayers in each townland.

16 Hardinge, 'Earliest known manuscript census', p. 317 n.   17 R.I.A. 23F23–38. 18 Hardinge, 'Earliest known manuscript census' p. 317.   19 Ibid., p. 326.   20 R.C. Simington, 'A "Census" of Ireland, *c.*1659 – the term "Titulado"' in *Analecta Hibernica*, xii (1943), pp 177–8.   21 Ibid., p. 177.

At the end of the entry for each barony the principal Irish names and their numbers are given. It should be noted that the *actual* poll-tax returns (that is the listing of the names of those who paid the poll-tax and the amount they paid) have not survived with the exception of those for four parishes in County Tyrone (Aghaloo, Donaghedy, Urney and Termonmaguirk)[22] and that the poll-tax summary *only* lists the aggregate number of tax payers, and the number of Irish and English taxpayers in the various townlands, parishes and baronies.

For most counties aggregate figures are also given for each barony. Unfortunately the returns for Counties Cavan, Galway, Mayo, Tyrone and Wicklow are missing as are returns for nine of Meath's twelve baronies (only Duleek, Skreen and Ratoath are available) and for four Cork baronies (Duhallow, Fermoy, Muskerry and Imokilly). For some other counties there are less serious omissions, with returns not available, for instance, for eight of Sligo's forty-one parishes.[23] Despite these deficiencies William Smyth has argued that 'once its limitations are recognised and other sources of evidence are used in conjunction with it – the '1659 Census' provides an enormous stimulus to our understanding of the complex cultural worlds of late medieval/early modern Ireland'.[24]

Considering the details that are outlined in Table 5 it is not altogether surprising that Hardinge would have presumed the returns to be a census. In reality the number of English, Scottish and Irish poll-tax payers in a townland or a list of the principal Irish names in a barony is not the sort of information that one would expect tax collectors to be interested in recording. Certainly no other extant Irish taxation return, either preceding or following this roll, contains such data. Furthermore, because the column showing the number of taxpayers is entitled 'Numb[er] of people' one could hardly fault Hardinge for mistakenly believing the taxation summary to be a census return.

In the 1930s the Irish Manuscripts Commission published this poll-tax summary under the title *A census of Ireland, circa 1659*, edited by Seamus Pender, and copies are available in most county libraries. At the time of publication a

---

22 P.R.O.N.I., T. 458/8 for Aghaloo; P.R.O.N.I., T. 808/15089 (N.L.I., p. 206) for Donaghedy and Urney; Earl Belmore, *The history of two Ulster manors* (London, 1881), pp 305–9 for Termonmaguirk. Note that the Aghaloo and Termonmaguirk lists are listings of those who paid the second poll-tax, which was presumably levied in late 1660. The 1660 poll-tax summary is an abstract of the returns from the first poll-tax. The returns for Donaghedy and Urney are undated and may be lists from the first poll-tax as they have significantly higher numbers of single people (11.9 per cent and 18.4 per cent respectively) than do the returns for Aghaloo (6.2 per cent) and Termonmaguirk (1.2 per cent). See S.T. Carleton, *Heads and hearths: the hearth money rolls and poll tax returns for Co. Antrim* (Belfast, 1991), p. 176. Also available is a 1661 (third) poll-tax listing for Clonmel town, South Tipperary Museum, Clonmel.   **23** 'Seventeenth-century hearth money rolls with the full transcript relating to County Sligo', ed. Edward MacLysaght in *Analecta Hibernica*, xxiv (1967), p. 3 (hereinafter 'Hearth money rolls', ed. MacLysaght). **24** Smyth, 'Society and settlement', p. 55.

debate was ongoing over whether the source was a census return or a taxation summary. The owner of the returns, the marquess of Lansdowne, had informed Hardinge that he believed the returns to be a census and noted that 'the returns are not copies, as they are in different hands. They were probably made by Petty's surveyors on the spot; nobody else would have been in a position to collect the figures.'[25] Pender also believed the returns to have been a census whilst his contemporary in the Irish Manuscripts Commission, Robert Simington, argued that the returns originated from a poll-tax.[26]

The debate over the origin of the returns was not conclusively settled until 1943 when W. J. Pilsworth published a short article in which he convincingly argued that 'the balance of probability lay' with it being 'a summarised form of the Poll Tax Returns for 1660'.[27] Pilsworth dated the returns to between January and 29 May of that year.[28] Fortunately, although Pender had believed the returns to be a census, he nonetheless replicated the poll-tax ordinances for 1660 and 1661 in an appendix to *Census of Ireland*, wherein it can be seen that the tax was levied 'For the speedy raising of/Moneys towards the Supply of the,/Army:/and for defraying of other/PUBLICK CHARGES./April the 24. 1660'.[29]

In retrospect, it is unfortunate that Pender chose the title *Census of Ireland* when publishing the taxation returns as this title has helped perpetuate Hardinge's initial misconception regarding the nature and purpose of the data. However, no serious historians today doubt that what Hardinge and Pender viewed as a census was actually a townland-by-townland summary of the number and ethnicity of those who paid the poll-tax in 1660. Thus, if one wishes to use the poll-tax returns as a means to derive a population estimate for an area for 1660 it is necessary to use a multiplier to convert the poll-tax figures into a total population figure. The magnitude of this multiplier and the likely errors inherent in the data will be discussed in greater detail in the following chapter.

Despite widespread agreement among scholars with respect to the origin of the taxation summary, a number of unanswered questions regarding the data remain. Most importantly the reason for the inclusion of 'census' type data in the taxation summary is unknown. The Cromwellian Wars had strained the public finances greatly during the 1650s and paying army arrears was vital for domestic stability. Thus, if the function of the tax was to raise revenue for an exchequer badly in need of funding, one would not expect extra expense to have been incurred in determining the ethnic breakdown of the taxpayers. There is nothing in the poll-tax ordinance that required the calculation of the ethnic aggregates, thus begging the questions, who authorised or ordered the tax collectors to make this determination and for what purpose was the information to be used?

These and other outstanding questions regarding the poll-tax notwithstanding, the data are a very important source for the demographic historian. The 1660

---

25 *Census Ire., 1659*, pp i–ii.   **26** Ibid., p. v.   **27** W.J. Pilsworth, 'Census or poll-tax' in *J.R.S.A.I.*, lxxiii (1943), pp 22–4.   **28** Ibid, p. 23.   **29** *Census Ire., 1659*, p. 610.

poll-tax was similar in form to a contemporary tax that was payable in England and charged a progressively increasing fee which was determined by rank or status. The Irish payments were significantly less than those charged in England, however. Anybody wishing to use the poll-tax as a demographic source is advised to read the 1660 poll-tax ordinance, tedious and verbose as it may be, towards the back of Pender's book as this will ensure that some of the mistakes commonly made when using the data can be avoided.[30] In summary, the ordinance outlines the charges accruing to each and every citizen in the country:

- The tax was to be paid by 'every person above the age of fifteen [i.e. those who had reached the age of fifteen], of either sex, of what degree or quality soever'. If a person was absent at the time of the tax, the sum was still due.
- Payments schedule was 12*d.* for every person under degree of yeoman or farmer and for his wife/widow; 2*s.* for every person under degree of gentleman or gentlewoman; 4*s.* for every person under degree of esquire and for his wife/ widow; 10*s.* for every person under degree of knight and for his wife/widow; 20*s.* for every person under degree of baronet or his wife/widow; 30*s.* for every person under degree of baron or his wife/widow; £4 for every person under degree of viscount or his wife/widow; £5 for every person under degree of earl, countess or countess dowager; £6 for every person under degree of marquess, marchioness or marchioness dowager; £8 for every person of degree of marquess, marchioness or marchioness dowager.
- There were no exemptions for either married or single women. Husbands were responsible for the tax due on their wives or children.
- Servants were *not* exempt. It was 'lawfull for every Master or Mistress to defaulk [default/deduct] such sum or sums of money as he or she shall pay by virtue of this Ordinance for their servants out of such wages as are or shall hereafter grow due to the servants'.[31]

The method of collecting the tax is also outlined:

- Commissioners were appointed for the counties, cities and boroughs for the purpose of organising the execution of the ordinance.
- The commissioners were to instruct a number of 'able and discrete Protestants' to appear for the purpose of executing the ordinance. A penalty of 40*s.* could be charged if those instructed didn't appear. These 'Protestants' were to report to the commissioners 'the Names and Sirnames, [*sic*] and qualifications of every person [of fifteen years and over] residing within the limits of the places'. Commissioners were to outline the charges on each person.[32]

---

30 Ibid., pp 610–27.   31 Ibid., pp 610, 612.   32 Ibid., pp 620–7, 613.

- If a person tried to avoid the tax, they were to be charged at triple their rate.
- Commissioners were to deliver to certain 'sufficient and substantial Inhabitants' lists of potential taxpayers and their associated charges. These substantial inhabitants were responsible for collecting the tax or in the case of non payment, goods to the value of the tax due.
- Commissioners were also to appoint a high-collector and to deliver lists of potential taxpayers and their associated charges to the high collector. The high collector was responsible for the whole sum and was bound to pay double the sum for his area if he failed to deliver the money. The high collector was to select the days when the tax was paid to them.
- If a taxpayer defaulted, goods and lands of an equivalent value were to be seized. If a collector died his heirs became responsible for completing the collection.
- On payment of the tax the tax payer received a 'Ticquet' [*sic*] expressing their name, qualification and the amount paid.
- Arthur Annesley Esq. was appointed treasurer for receiving the tax. High collectors were to periodically present payments to Annesley. Annesley was to pay the army with the monies received as specified by the committee, consisting of Lord Broghill, Sir Charles Coot[e] and Sir William Bury.
- Those exempted from the tax were the provost, fellows and scholars of the College of the Holy Trinity (T.C.D.), church ministers, their wives and unmarried children less than fifteen and their dependant family and hospitalmen or those dependent on alms.

PRE-CENSUS POPULATION SOURCES – THE HEARTH-TAX

In the discussion on pre-census Irish demographic analysis in the first chapter it was seen that total housing numbers, originating from the returns made by the hearth-money collectors, were the basis for the majority of national population estimates made before the commencement of statutory censuses in the nineteenth century. A tax on hearths was introduced in England in 1661 and the Irish parliament passed an Act, 14 & 15 Car. II, *c*.17, in 1662 which introduced a hearth-tax in Ireland. The tax arose from the Crown's need to replace the feudal tenures that were abolished following the Restoration of Charles II in 1660, effectively shifting tax charges from landowners to the general population and particularly to the poorer classes.[33]

The 1662 Act provided for the annual payment of 2*s*. per hearth, payable in two equal instalments on 25 March (Lady Day) and 29 September (Michaelmas), with the first 1*s*. payment due on 25 March 1663. The method for collecting the tax invested responsibility for determining the number of hearths in each house with the parish constable who was assisted by two 'persons of good repute',

33 'Hearth money rolls of County Louth', ed. McNeill, p. 80.

appointed at the quarter sessions following Michaelmas day.[34] Each householder was required to present the appointed persons with a written account of the number of hearths within his or her house by 20 December of each year. The appointed persons were then required to verify the received accounts by entering into each house to count the number of fixed hearths. They subsequently forwarded the verified returns to the justice of peace for their county. The clerk of the peace prepared a duplicate copy of the returns and sent one to the court of exchequer and one to the county sheriff.[35] The sheriff was responsible for arranging the collection of the tax and for paying the collected monies to the exchequer.[36] The geographic area covered by a tax collector was termed a 'walk'.

Exemptions from the tax were granted to buildings that were not private residences, to persons dependent on alms or unable to gain a living from work and to householders whose house and property failed to meet certain minimum values.[37] It would appear that these exemption criteria were too broad as amending legislation was introduced in 1665 to close some loopholes in the law that had become apparent. This legislation became effective in the tax year 1666–7.[38] As a consequence of this amendment, the minimum property qualifications were limited to widows only and houses with no fixed hearth were to be charged at the two-hearth rate of 4s. This restricted exemption on property values continued until 1687 when *all* houses of less than 8s. value were again exempted from the tax.[39] The amendment also made the tax payable in one lump sum on 10 January, with hearth-number returns to be delivered to the collectors by 10 November previously.[40] The first payment under this amending legislation was due on 10 January 1667.

A very important change was also introduced in relation to the method of collecting the tax. As already described, prior to the amending Act the tax was collected directly by public servants. The amending legislation allowed for the 'farming' out of the tax collection process, which effectively meant that the hearth-tax collection rights were auctioned to the highest bidder who was then responsible for collecting the tax. Farming of the tax continued until 1705–6 when direct collection was reintroduced.[41] This amending Act expanded the tax base significantly and resulted in a greater proportion of the population being required to pay the tax. The original Act and the official summary of the 1665 amendment are replicated in MacLysaght's introductory note to the 1665 Sligo roll, published in *Analecta Hibernica*.[42] If one studies the Act, it is easy to comprehend contemporary comments about how those taxed viewed the hearth-tax with absolute contempt.[43] The obligation on the collector to enter a

34 'Hearth money rolls', ed. MacLysaght, p. 6.   **35** Ibid., p. 7.   **36** Ibid., pp 8–9. **37** Ibid., pp 10, 12.   **38** Carleton, *Heads and hearths*, p. xii.   **39** MacLysaght, 'Seventeenth-century hearth rolls', p. 16.   **40** Ibid., pp 13–14.   **41** Cullen, 'Population trends in seventeenth-century Ireland', p. 151.   **42** 'Hearth money rolls', ed. MacLysaght, pp 5–14.   **43** A commentator in 1780 described the tax in the following fashion: 'The

person's house to verify the householder's returns was considered particularly objectionable and it was this intrusion into the privacy of the home that was cited as a reason for abolishing the tax in England in the aftermath of the Williamite wars (1688).[44] Nonetheless, the tax was maintained in Ireland, albeit in greatly modified form after 1793, until 1824.

Despite the aversion to the hearth-tax felt by those on whom it was imposed, the demographic historian is fortunate that this particular tax was introduced as surviving hearth-rolls are one of the key Irish pre-census population sources. Unfortunately, as with so many demographic sources, the original rolls were destroyed in the P.R.O. explosion in 1922 and one is thus limited to using surviving transcripts of the rolls, which were made prior to the destruction of the originals. Typically the transcribed hearth-rolls date from the earliest years of the tax (most rolls are from the 1660s) and, with few exceptions, are only available for some Leinster and Ulster counties.

Essential readings for researchers interested in the origin and development of the hearth-tax are MacLysaght's introduction to the 1665 Sligo hearth-roll published in *Analecta Hibernica* in 1967 and Charles McNeill's introduction to the 1663 Drogheda roll published in the *Journal of the County Louth Archaeological Society* in 1925.[45] More recently, S.T. Carleton has written a useful introduction to the hearth-tax and the 1660 poll-tax in his examination of the poll-tax and hearth-money returns for County Antrim, entitled *Heads and hearths*.[46] Carleton's summary of the results of his analysis of the hearth and poll-tax data is also worth reading.[47] A sample hearth-tax roll for the 1666–7 tax year for Drangan parish, County Tipperary is shown in Figure 2.

The amending legislation introduced in 1665 is of particular importance to the demographic historian. The most important changes in this legislation from a demographic point of view were the farming of the tax and the imposition of a double charge on houses with no fixed hearths. David Dickson *et al* have

---

taxes in Ireland are moderate ... There is one, however, repugnant to liberty and oppressive in its exercise. This is a tax upon hearths (£55,000 annually). A tax which gives a right of entry into the inmost recesses of the house; and which alarming the unfortunate cottier, as if a foreign enemy was at the door, hurries him into the field with the few moveables [sic] he can convey from the relentless collector. William the III abolished this odious tax in England, upon his accession. It would have been a judicious measure, if this benefit had been extended to Ireland', *View of the present state of Ireland containing observations upon the following subjects, viz. ... effect of the present mode of raising the revenue ...* (1780), pp 80–1. **44** When the tax was abandoned in England, it was described as 'not only a great oppressor of the poorer sort, but a badge of slavery upon the whole people, exposing every man's house to be entered into and searched at pleasure by persons unknown to him', 'Hearth money rolls of County Louth', ed. McNeill, pp 80–1. **45** 'Hearth money rolls', ed. MacLysaght, pp 1–16; 'Hearth money rolls of County Louth', ed. McNeill, pp 79–82. **46** Carleton, *Heads and hearths*, pp xi–xv. **47** Ibid., pp 175–87.

Figure 2. Sample page from 1666–7 hearth-roll for part of Drangan parish,
County Tipperary

			Hths.	s.
PARISHES OF ST. JOHNSTOWNE				
AND COOLEAGH—Continued.				
Killbridie			Hths.	s.
Patrick St. John	*n*	...	1	2
James Codie	*n*	...	1	2
John Crowlie	*n*	...	1	2
William St. John	*n*	...	1	2
Walter St. John	*n*	...	1	2

PARISH OF DRANGANE.

Drangane

Nicholas Daie	*n*	...	2	4
William Millett	*n*	...	1	2
Henry James	*n*	...	1	2
John Carroll	*n*	...	1	2
Richard Mongaine	*n*	...	1	2
John Hogaine	*n*	...	1	2
John Dwylloagh	*n*	...	1	2
John Derregane	*n*	...	1	2
Onor Morrishee	*n*	...	1	2
Edmond Crockayne	*n*	...	1	2
Dermod Dwilloagh	*n*	...	1	2
John Meagher	*n*	1 & a forge	4	
Richard Shea	*n*	...	1	2
Edmond Kelly	*n*	...	1	2
Thomas Meagher	*n*	...	1	2
Edmond Hogaine	*n*	...	1	2
Teige Damechair	*n*	...	1	2
Margarett Carroll	*n*	...	1	2
William Cahessie	*n*	...	1	2
Nicholas Edin	*n*	...	1	2
William Hickey	*n*	...	1	2
James Hickey	*n*	...	1	2
Thomas Kelly	*n*	...	1	2
Jane Green	*n*	...	1	2
Jane Cahessey	*n*	...	1	2

Preistowne

Donnogh Kearney	*n*	...	1	2
James Stapleton	*n*	...	1	2
Edmond Cantwell	*n*	...	1	2
Edmond Stoake	*n*	...	1	2
Keadagh Kelly	*n*	...	1	2
Richard Tobin	*n*	...	1	2
John Brenane	*n*	...	1	2
Walter Tobin	*n*	...	1	2
Edmond Fanninge	*n*	...	1	2
Thomas Meagher	*n*	...	1	2
Katherine Meagher	*n*	...	1	2
Ellin Nash	*n*	...	1	2
Jnane Croake	*n*	...	1	2

Cloneshea

Margarett Shea	*n*	...	1	2
James Breningham	*n*	...	1	2
John Henis	*n*	...	1	2
Edmond Meagher	*n*	...	1	2
Thomas Bryen	*n*	...	1	2
John Bryen	*n*	...	1	2
James Shortell	*n*	...	1	2
Richard Henis	*n*	...	1	2
John McMoragh	*n*	...	1	2

Ballynenaine

James Hennis	*n*	...	1	2
John Hogane	*n*	...	1	2
Henry Meade	*n*	...	1	2
James Tobin	*n*	...	1	2
Teig Hennisse	*n*	...	1	2
Morrish Fanning	*n*	...	1	2
John Quidihie	*n*	...	1	2
William Birne	*n*	...	1	2
Margarett Kelly	*n*	...	1	2
Katherine Meagher	*n*	...	1	2
Thomas Naishe	*n*	...	1	2
Thomas Kelly	*n*	...	1	2
Teige Kelly	*n*	...	1	2
William Bourke	*n*	...	1	2
John McHugh	*n*	...	1	2
William Hennis	*n*	...	1	2
Walter Landers	*n*	...	1	2
Thomas Dongan	*n*	...	1	2
Teige Brien	*n*	...	1	2
John Wale	*n*	...	1	2
Katherine Tobin	*n*	...	1	2
Austas Boine	*n*	...	1	2

Newtowne

Thomas Meagher	*n*	...	1	2
Thomas McRory	*n*	...	1	2
Richard Meagher	*n*	...	1	2
James Dunigh	*n*	...	1	2
John Meagher	*n*	...	1	2
William Mackey	*n*	...	1	2
Connor Meagher	*n*	...	1	2
Phillipp Shehaine	*n*	...	1	2
Edmond Fanninge	*n*	...	1	2
Derby Phelane	*n*	...	1	2
Connor Kissyn	*n*	...	1	2
John Shea	*n*	...	1	2
William Walsh	*n*	...	1	2

Mogowry

John Carran	*n*	...	1	2
Teige Meagher	*n*	...	1	2
William Dwynn	*n*	...	1	2
Edmond Dwynn	*n*	...	1	2
John McWilliam	*n*	...	1	2
Phillipp Meagher	*n*	...	1	2

(107)

(Source: Laffan, *Tipperary's families,* p. 107).

suggested that this two-hearth penalty for houses with no hearths may have been responsible for speeding the diffusion of the chimney in Irish vernacular architecture[48] as the addition of a fixed hearth in a non-hearth house would have reduced the family's hearth-tax burden by 50 per cent. However, it would seem probable that the doubling of the tax for non-hearth houses would not have been applied too rigorously and would more probably have been used as an incentive to encourage the households to pay the charge for a single hearth. As late as 1813 in north Donegal, for instance, it was noted that 'The cottages ... seldom have a chimney, they are almost always full of smoke'.[49]

The farming of the tax, on the other hand, is likely to have had a more im-mediate impact on the general population. When state officials were responsible for collecting the tax, as was the case between 1662 and 1666, there was no monetary incentive for the officials to collect the tax assiduously. However, when the tax was farmed and private individuals were paying substantial sums for the rights to collect it, it followed that the more tax that was collected, the greater the profit that accrued to the tax farmer. County figures for the purchase of the farm rights are available for a number of years between 1672 and 1700 (see appendix A) and these can be used to form general impressions as to the completeness of county hearth-rolls. The actual amount of money paid for the rights to collect the county hearth-tax was influenced by a number of factors, the most important of which was the extent of competition for the collection rights. Obviously the more people in the market for the rights to collect the tax, the higher the price paid at the auction and *vice versa*. Of course the tax-farmer purchased the rights with the intention of making some profit on the transaction and so the ultimate factor determining this price was the potential revenue that would accrue to him. It can, therefore, be presumed that the maximum sum that an individual would have been prepared to pay for the collection rights would have been the anticipated net collection revenue (total revenue with collection expenses deducted) minus a sum that the farmer viewed as his minimum acceptable profit. In Table 6 the amount of tax collected according to some county hearth-rolls is compared with the sum paid at farm auctions in 1672 and 1682. This basic comparison clearly shows that, as could be expected, the pre-amendment rolls were significantly more deficient than were the post-amendment rolls . It seems as if the County Dublin roll for 1664 is surprisingly complete in comparison with the other pre-amendment rolls, with the tax collected being 86 per cent of the cost of the 1672 farm but this may have been a result of a lack of competition for the Dublin farm as by 1684, the cost of the Dublin county collection rights had increased to £750 – from £608 in 1682.

---

48 Dickson, Ó Gráda and Daultrey, 'Hearth tax', pp 139–40.   **49** Mason, *A statistical account or parochial survey of Ireland*, ii, p. 156.

Table 6. Revenue in county rolls compared with county
farm totals for 1672 and 1682

County	Year	Revenue in roll) (£-s	1672 farm (£)	1682 farm (£)	Roll as % of 1672 farm revenue	Roll as % of 1682 farm revenue
Compiled under original legislation of 1662						
Antrim	1666	496–08	1353	1620	36.69%	30.64%
Armagh	1664	251–08	517	567	48.63%	44.34%
Dublin city	1664	828–04	1620	2365	51.12%	35.02%
Dublin co.	1664	528–18	610	608	86.70%	86.99%
Donegal	1665	358–12	605	880	59.27%	40.75%
Monaghan	1663	173–08	355	379	48.85%	45.75%
Monaghan	1665	137–10	355	379	38.73%	36.28%
Tipperary	1666	730–10	1298	1506	56.28%	48.51%
Tyrone	1666	324–16	563	868	57.69%	37.42%
Compiled under 1665 amending legislation						
Antrim	1669	1148–16	1353	1620	84.91%	70.91%
Tipperary	1667	1274–06	1298	1506	98.17%	84.61%
Wicklow (pt. of)	1668	401–00	457	570	87.75%	70.35%

(Sources: Armagh, *Arch. Hib.*, viii (1936), p. 202; Dublin city, *D.K.P.R.I.*, lvii (1936), pp 559–60; Dublin County, *J.C.K.A.S.*, xi (1930–3), p. 406; Donegal, P.R.O.N.I., T. 307; Monaghan, Denis C. Rushe, *History of Monaghan* (Monaghan, 1996 repr.) pp 291–338; Antrim, Carleton, *Heads and hearths* (Belfast, 1991), p. 191, Tipperary, Thomas Laffan, *Tipperary's Families* (Dublin, 1911), p. 73 and pp 74–193 (1667 figures include 541 illegible entries); Tyrone, Earl Belmore, *The history of two Ulster manors* (London, 1881), p. 315; Wicklow, *J.R.S.A.I*, lxi (1931), pp 165–78; Farm revenues, T.C.D. MS. 883, i, p. 73.

As the amount paid for the collection rights included provision for a certain profit for the tax-farmer, the rolls are more deficient than the percentage figures shown in Table 6. The typical profit made by the farmers is unknown but it is likely to have been in the order of 10 per cent. In addition the tax-farmer had to meet collection expenses out of the collected revenue and Dickson *et al.* have estimated typical expenses to be also of the order of 10 per cent of the net return.[50] Thus the total collected revenues (Y) can be estimated at:

$$Y = 1.25 \times (\text{price paid for the collection rights})[51]$$

50 Dickson, Ó Gráda and Daultrey, 'Hearth tax', p. 158.　**51** $Y = P + E + \Pi$ where Y is total revenue collected, P is price paid at farm auction, E is collection expenses and Π is

It is likely that the degree of underestimation in the number of houses was less than the underestimation in the number of hearths and is also probable that more remote areas were less intensely taxed than more accessible districts. Nonetheless, it does seem that the typical 1660s hearth-roll is not a very accurate estimator of the total number of houses in an area.

Earlier it was presumed that the 1665 amending legislation spread the tax burden more widely across the population and that the enumeration of houses and hearths increased as loopholes in the original legislation were closed. Certainly, if the new rules were applied rigorously, an increase in the numbers paying the tax would have been an inevitable consequence. There are only two counties for which transcripts of rolls compiled both before and after the introduction of the amending legislation have survived;[52] the rolls dating from 1666 and 1669 for Antrim and rolls from 1666 and 1667 for Tipperary. From this very limited information it is clear that the 1665 amendment significantly broadened the tax base and boosted the amount of tax paid as a result. The hearths and houses figures for these two counties and for Dunleer parish, County Louth and Monkstown union, County Dublin, are shown in Table 7.

Table 7. Comparison between pre- and post-amendment hearth-rolls for Counties Antrim and Tipperary and Dunleer parish, County Louth and Monkstown union, County Dublin. Tipperary 1667 figures include 541 illegible entries.

County	Pre-amendment		Post-amendment		% increase in	
	Houses	£	Houses	£	Houses	£
Antrim (1666 & 1669)	4649	496.4	10137	1148.8	118.0%	131.4%
Tipperary (1666 & 1667)	6605	730.5	11488	1274.3	73.93%	74.44%
Dunleer (1664 & 1667)	N/A	5.6	N/A	7.4	N/A	32.1%
Monkstown (1664 & 1667)	205	22.6	236	29.7	15.1%	31.4%

Clearly there was a substantial increase in the number of houses paying the tax in both Antrim and Tipperary following the 1665 amending legislation. Although information is not available for other areas, it seems probable that more households

profit to the farmer. If we assume that ($\Pi = E = (Y \times 0\cdot1)$) then $Y = 1\cdot25 \times P$. **52** A 1664 abstract and a copy of the 1667 roll for Dunleer parish, County Louth and a 1664 and 1667 roll for Monkstown union, County Dublin, also exist.

were drawn into the tax net throughout the country. It can therefore be confidently concluded that while all tax-rolls may be deficient to some degree, rolls that date from the 1666/7 tax year onwards are probably less so.[53]

It is also likely that the farming of the tax resulted in people in more remote areas being dragged into the tax net. This is because state officials would have been less diligent in collecting the tax from the more remote districts on their 'walks',[54] whereas under the system of tax farming, the high price paid for the collection rights provided added impetus to venture into more isolated parts. There is some evidence to suggest that this may be the case.[55] From the county farm revenues for various years in the late seventeenth century (appendix A), it can be shown that the aggregate farm revenue for the counties along the western seaboard, many of whose inhabitants lived in outlying areas, increased by 28.8 per cent between 1672 and 1682. During the same period the aggregate revenue for the rest of the country increased by only 19.8 per cent. By contrast, the aggregate revenue for the eastern seaboard counties, typically well intersected by arteries of communications and where it was easier to impose taxation, increased by 19.2 per cent whilst for the rest of the country the increase was 22.9 per cent. It seems likely, therefore, that there was a strong bias towards taxing the population in more accessible parts of a region and that their counterparts in remote areas were more rigorously taxed during the farming periods. Thus, on a localised scale, even the pre-amendment hearth rolls can be presumed to estimate more accurately housing numbers in accessible regions than in more remote regions.

On a related point, it is possible that the loopholes in the original legislation provided an escape route for an ever-increasing number of potential taxpayers between 1662 and 1665. Consider the case of County Monaghan, for instance. Rolls exist for that county for the years 1663 and 1665 respectively, both of which were compiled under the original rules. The 1663 roll contains 1,748 names while that of 1665 contains 1,391 names, a decline of more than 20 per cent. Furthermore, over 850 names on the 1665 list do not occur on the earlier roll which means that of the 1,748 names on the 1663 roll, only about 550 names (31 per cent) recur in the roll compiled two years later.[56] Whilst it is hard

---

53 Rolls dated 1666 were for Michaelmas 1666 and would thus have been compiled in December 1665 under the original legislation. Rolls for 1667 were the first rolls compiled under the 1665 amending legislation.   **54** In the more remote districts it is likely that the collector had to agree a tax level with the inhabitants rather than taxing every hearth – 'The number of Roman Catholics are here underrated for the hearth-money collectors, in the wild uncultivated mountains [of Kerry], are obliged to compound for this tax, and take a certain sum for many cabins, otherwise they would collect nothing', Charles Smith, *The ancient and present state of the County of Kerry* (Dublin, 1979 repr.), pp 252–3 n.   **55** Note in Table 7 that there was only a small difference between the pre- and post-amendment hearth-tax figures for Dunleer and Monkstown compared with the figures for Counties Tipperary and Antrim.   **56** Denis Carolan Rushe, *History of Monaghan for two hundred years, 1660–1860* (Monaghan, 1996, repr.), p. 4.

to imagine that tax evasion on this scale was occurring and scrutiny of the two rolls suggests that the 1665 list was poorly recorded, this disparity does raise the possibility of a general decline in the effectiveness of the imposition of the tax prior to the passage of the amending legislation.[57] Carleton has similarly noted that the 1666 hearth-roll for Tyrone was more defective than the 1664 roll.[58]

Surviving hearth-roll transcripts are located in P.R.O.N.I. (rolls for eight of the nine Ulster counties – Down is the only Ulster county for which there are no surviving hearth-rolls), the N.L.I. and the N.A.I. In addition, many public libraries have acquired copies of the rolls pertaining to their particular county for their local history collections. Hayes' *Manuscripts sources* and *Manuscript sources: articles in Irish periodicals* can be used to locate many of the surviving transcripts and published hearth-tax lists and in appendix B, the location of published hearth-rolls and hearth-tax abstracts are listed. In working with transcriptions of the hearth-rolls it is advisable to apply checks to the transcribed data. It is useful, for instance, to count the total number of hearths oneself and thereafter to compare this sum with either the total number of hearths or the total amount of money collected if this information is recorded at the foot of the transcription. If two or more separately copied transcripts exist, one can also compare the rolls to see if errors in one roll can be corrected by reference to the data in another.

The hearth-tax data, of course, is not a census *per se* but an enumeration of householders who paid the hearth-tax. To convert the hearth-money figures to population estimates, therefore, one is required to estimate the proportion of the total number of households that avoided the tax and, summing this figure with the number of paying households, multiply the estimate for the *total number of houses* by an 'average household size' figure. The method of converting a 'houses taxed' figure to a 'population' estimate will be discussed in detail in the next chapter.

PRE-CENSUS POPULATION SOURCES – RELIGIOUS CENSUSES

Ireland experienced a demographic revolution during the seventeenth century, which saw the political and religious balance in the country undergo fundamental change. Ulster was metamorphosed from being the most 'native' province at the beginning of the century to being the most 'non-native' by the end of the Cromwellian period and there were many Protestants who wished that this revolution would be extended throughout Ireland.[59] A consequence of the

---

57 For Monaghan parish, for instance, in 1663, 87 houses paid tax for 177 hearths but two years later 102 houses paid tax for only 114 hearths. There are numerous problems like this in the rolls. 58 Carleton, *Heads and hearths*, p. 177. 59 *Census Ire., 1659*, pp xiii–xvii. Of course, this changing demographic makeup in Ulster continued after the 1660s. For a comment on the use of the 1660 poll-tax for Ulster population study see *Sources for the study of local history in Northern Ireland* (Belfast, 1968), p. 35.

growth of Protestantism in Ireland during the seventeenth and eighteenth centuries was that a number of wide-ranging inquiries into the religious breakdown of the country were conducted, particularly during the eighteenth century, at both local and national level. Parliamentary committees were the primary driving force behind these inquiries and responsibility for gathering the statistics was often, though not exclusively, invested in the hearth-money collectors.

The first series of these religious censuses were held in the early 1730s. In 1731 a census was organised at diocese level (coinciding with an attempt to disarm papists) with the enumeration undertaken by the parish ministers, and some parish data has survived by virtue of it being copied before the loss of the original records in 1922. A parliamentary inquiry into the 'state of popery', focussing on the number and condition of Catholic chapels, the number of priests and friars and the state of Catholic education, was also initiated in that year.[60] The most complete material from the 1731 census is the parish data for County Kilkenny. Copies of the original data were made available to William Tighe when he was writing his *Statistical observations relative to the county of Kilkenny* and in this book he lists the number of inhabitants, the number of people above 60 years of age and below 10 years of age and the number of Protestants and Protestant families in each Ossory parish in the county in 1731. Tighe also recorded contemporary population figures (1799–1800) against which the 1731 figures can be compared.[61]

There is a substantial body of 1731 data (typically only showing the total number of Protestant and Catholic families in a parish) in the various 'succession lists' published in the first half of the twentieth century, with Ossory diocese (which includes much of County Kilkenny) being particularly well covered. The principal force behind the production of these succession-list publications was Canon James Leslie who published lists for the dioceses of Ardfert and Aghadoe, Armagh, Clogher, Derry, Ferns, Raphoe and Ossory among others.[62] Leslie's lists follow a standard format, naming the Protestant ministers at various points in time and other relevant parish information. Parish population data, if featured in these publications, usually appear in the 'Notes' section, which typically completes the entry for each individual parish. The following extract from the note for the parish of Charlestown, County Louth is characteristic of the data to be found in Leslie's works:

> In 1662 church and chancel were ruinous. In 1633 Lord Louth was impropriator; value £8. In 1692 'Brabazon Moore, impropriator, church

---

60 'State of Popery (Ulster)' in *Arch. Hib.*, i, pp 10–27; 'State of Popery: Munster' in *Arch. Hib.*, ii, pp 108–56; 'State of Popery' in *Arch. Hib.*, iii, pp 124–59 for Connaught; 'State of Popery' in *Arch. Hib.*, iv, pp 131–77 for Leinster.　**61** William Tighe, *Statistical observations relative to the county of Kilkenny made in the years 1800 & 1801* (Dublin, 1802), pp 456–8. **62** James B. Leslie, *History of Kilsaran* (Dundalk, 1908), p. 204. Also, see bibliography for listing of various published succession-lists.

out of repair; Moore refuses to repair chancel. The body was covered with slates, no bell. Thomas Stephens and James Akin, Churchwardens; James Matthews, Popish Priest, here 7 years ; no meeting house or mass house.' In 1731 Vicar was 'resident, but had no parsonage house' (*Parl. Ret.*). In 1764 90 Protestants, 555 Roman Catholics, 1 church and no chapel in the parish (*Hearth Money Return*).[63]

Other succession lists have been published by the Revd Michael Comerford (Kildare and Leighlin), R.H. Rennison (Waterford and Lismore) and Revd St John D. Seymour (Cashel and Emly), all of which contain some pre-census materials.[64] Comerford's lists are particularly useful as they feature data from the 1730s and from various censuses conducted during the 1760s. These published succession lists can be found in the N.L.I., the R.C.B. Library and the various university libraries in Ireland. County libraries will usually have a copy of the lists pertaining to their particular area.

In 1732 another religious census, aimed at enumerating families rather than people, was held. This time, responsibility for gathering the statistics was vested in the hearth-money collectors. Whether it was dissatisfaction with results of the 1731 census or a desire to verify the results that led to another religious census being conducted the year after the 1731 census is not clear. Although the 1732 census provides the first data based on baronial divisions, unfortunately, it does not require more than a cursory glance at the returns to raise one's suspicions about the accuracy of this census as some baronies are recorded under the wrong counties and figures for many areas are wanting. Nonetheless, the importance of this return stems from the provision of baronial 'family' figures, the first time that data such as this were recorded in a national inquiry since the 1660 poll-tax.

The county figures were published (reputedly) by David Bindon in 1736 in a pamphlet entitled *An abstract of the number of Protestant and Popish families*[65] and the manuscript containing the baronial figures is available in the Lambeth Palace Library and a microfilm copy is available in P.R.O.N.I.[66] If the barony figures are used in conjunction with Bindon's published abstract, and provided care is taken to ensure that any figures included in the wrong counties are redistributed, the barony figures are a useful, if greatly under-utilised, source. The 1732 baronial data have been used by David Dickson to study the evolution of Protestantism

63 James B. Leslie, *Armagh clergy and parishes* (Dundalk, 1911), p. 176.   **64** Comerford, *Kildare and Leighlin*, i, pp 261–74 and iii, pp 404–7; Revd St John D. Seymour, *The succession of the parochial clergy in the united diocese of Cashel and Emly* (Dublin, 1908), pp 101–2; R.H. Rennison, *Succession lists of the bishops, cathedral and parochial clergy of the dioceses of Waterford and Lismore* (n.p., 1920), pp 233–4.   **65** [Bindon?] *An abstract of the number of Protestant and Popish families in the several counties and provinces of Ireland*, pp 3–6. **66** Lambeth Palace Library, MS. 1742, ff 43–8 [P.R.O.N.I., Microfilm 310].

in Kerry during the eighteenth century and by Kerby Miller and Liam Kennedy to perform a similar exercise for County Longford.[67]

This interest in religious denomination figures proved pervasive as two years later, in 1734, a religious census was carried out in north Antrim. This census data has survived among the Bishop Reeves papers in T.C.D. and in the Seamus Uí Casaide papers in the National Library.[68] It records the name of each townland, its chief tenant and the name and religious denomination of each householder in the barony of Cary. Summary information is also available for the baronies of Dunluce and Killconway.[69] Much of the census has been published in recent volumes of *The Glynns* journal.[70]

The proliferation of censuses focussed on determining the religious break-down of part or all of the country in the 1730s is itself indicative of the concern felt by the Protestant authorities over the failure of the Penal Laws to significantly weaken Catholicism as well as anxiety that Stuart supporters might be preparing to recover Ireland. The following text by William Chetwood, a mid-eighteenth century traveller in Ireland, further testifies to this concern over the religious question:

> Your Lordship will find by this [tabulated presentation of the provincial aggregates for the 1731 religious census], that the Papists then exceeded the Protestants [by] 609315 [people]; but since the wise Legislature have caused so many Protestant Seminaries to be erected and endowed in different Parts of this Kingdom, where the Children of poor Roman Catholicks [*sic*] are brought up in the reformed Religion, that it is natural to suppose the Mass, by degrees, must lessen in its numerous Followers.[71]

Considering the contemporary mood among the Protestant elite it is not surprising to find that religious censuses were periodically conducted in the 1740s through to the 1760s, culminating in perhaps the most well-known of these censuses, that of 1766. The distrust and suspicion with which Protestants viewed Catholics stemmed from their minority position within the country and unease that Catholics were intent on regaining lands lost during the seventeenth

---

67 David Dickson, 'The 1732 religious returns and the evolution of Protestant Kerry' in *Journal of the Kerry Archeological and Historical Society*, xix (1986), pp 65–72; Liam Kennedy, Kerby A. Miller, with Mark Graham, 'The long retreat: Protestants, economy and society, 1660–1926' in Raymond Gillespie and Gerard Moran (eds), *Longford: essays in county history* (Dublin, 1991), pp 31–61. **68** A list of the householders in the Barony of Cary, 1734 coped from a record preserved among the Antrim papers at Glenarm (T.C.D., MS. 1059, pp 121–58); N.L.I., MS. 5456. **69** Number of householders in the Baronys of Dunluce, Cary and Kilconway (T.C.D., MS. 1059, p. 159). **70** *Journal of the Glens of Antrim Historical Society*, xxi (1993), pp 65–76; xxii (1994), pp 53–8 and xxv (1997), pp 30–7 for some Cary barony data. **71** William R. Chetwood, *A tour through Ireland in several entertaining letters . . . interspersed with observations on the manners, customs . . . of that*

century. Thus, any increased international tensions raised anxieties among Protestants that Catholics would be willing allies for their enemies.

In 1739 the Anglo-Spanish war (Jenkin's ear) broke out and Britain found herself engaged in a decade-long European war.[72] Following the outbreak of hostilities the Irish parliament moved, as was customary during periods of heightened tension, to disarm Catholics and the House of Lords requested on 24 March 1740 that a list of 'the Names of all Protestant Housekeepers' be compiled for the purpose of forming a militia, if circumstances so warranted.[73] The following day

> The Lord Chancellor acquainted the house, that in obedience to their Lordships' Ordered of Yesterday, he had waited upon his Grace the Lord Lieutenant with the Resolution and Address of this House, to desire his Grace would be pleased to give Directions to the proper Officers [the hearth-money collectors] to return to this House the Names of all Protestant House-keepers within their respective districts, distinguishing each County, Barony and parish, and his Grace was pleased to make this Answer, That he would give directions accordingly.[74]

Although this enumeration covered the entire island, the originals were destroyed in 1922 and all that remains is a brief abstract for the entire country[76] and transcriptions made by Tennison Groves, a professional searcher to whom contemporary demographic historians are greatly indebted,[75] for parts of Counties Antrim, Armagh, Derry, Donegal, Down and Tyrone – effectively the most Protestant parts of the country. These returns, containing the names of the householders, were arranged on a county, barony and parish basis and may be consulted in the P.R.O.N.I., the N.L.I. or the N.A.I.[77] A comparison of the 1740 and 1766 figures for the two County Tyrone parishes for which complete lists exist shows that in 1740, 74 names were recorded for Kildress and 170 for Derryloran whereas by 1766, the respective Protestant household figures were 172 (295 Catholic) and 419 (168 Catholic) households. That the 1766 figures, which included Presbyterians, are significantly larger than the 1740 figures would seem to suggest that the 1740 return included Church of Ireland members only. As the origin of this return is not widely known and the figures are often incorrectly used in research, the national abstract is replicated in Table 8.

country (1746), p. 199.   **72** Glyn Williams and John Ramsden, *Ruling Britannia: a political history of Britain 1688–1988* (London, 1990), pp 68–79.   **73** *I.H.L.J.*, iii (1727–52), p. 486. **74** Ibid., p. 488.   **75** Ríonach Ní Néill, 'Records of central and local government after 1700' in William Nolan and Anngret Simms (eds), *Irish towns: a guide to the sources* (Dublin, 1998), pp 98–9.   **76** National abstract in Edward Wakefield, *An account of Ireland statistical and political* (2 vols, London, 1812), ii, p. 586.   **77** P.R.O.N.I., T. 808/15258; G.O. 539; N.A.I., 1A 46 100.

Table 8. Abstract of 1740 Protestant householders returns

Survey	Protestant householders	Survey	Protestant householders
Antrim	19,100	Kilkenny	2,242
Armagh	11,415	Limerick	2,246
Athlone	1,936	Londonderry	14,404
Clare	1,455	Mayo	824
Cork	4,053	Philipstown	2,320
Donegal	9,523	Rathkeale	945
Drogheda	1,664	Sligo	1,457
Dublin	7,065	Waterford	1,521
Enniskillen	2,744	Wexford	2,343
Fermanagh	4,447	Wicklow	3,099
Kerry	1,264	**Total**	**96,067**

(Source, Edward Wakefield, *Account of Ireland*, ii, p. 586).

In 1744, by order of the House of Lords, the hearth-money collectors were again instructed to carry out a religious enumeration, this time being requested to aggregate the number of Protestants and papists and to record the number and condition of the various religious houses within the bounds of their 'walks'.[78] As this census was based on hearth-tax returns, it is likely that Protestants were overestimated in the census as will be shown in the next chapter. The only surviving material from this census is for parts of County Fermanagh (parish aggregates only), this data being available in the P.R.O.N.I. and reproduced in Leslie's *Clogher* succession list.[79]

It may have been noticed that a large proportion of the surviving religious census data covers various parts of Ulster while data for much of Connaught is, by contrast, scant. Fortunately this imbalance is redressed somewhat by the diocesan census conducted by the bishop of Elphin, Edward Synge, in 1749. Synge ordered his parish incumbents to gather data for a religious census of the diocese. The information collected by parish churchwardens covered all of the seventy-five parishes in the diocese, thereby encompassing most of County Roscommon and parts of eastern Sligo and eastern Galway.[80] The original census is retained in the National Archives and a partly transcribed copy is

78 *Sources for the study of local history in Northern Ireland* (Belfast, 1968), p. 35. **79** P.R.O.N.I., T. 808/15261; Leslie, *Clogher clergy and parishes*, pp 261–2; *Sources for the study of local history in Northern Ireland*, p. 41. **80** *The letters of Lord Chief Baron Edward Willes to the earl of Warwick, 1757–1762. An account of Ireland in the mid-eighteenth century*, ed. James Kelly (Aberystwyth, 1990), p. 95 (hereinafter *The letters of Lord Chief Baron Edward Willes*, ed. Kelly).

available in Roscommon county library.[81] This religious census is a formidable example of early modern enumeration and is the most comprehensive conducted in Ireland in the eighteenth century. It is somewhat surprising, therefore, that it has never been published (at the time of writing the Irish Manuscripts Commission is considering a proposal to publish the census), that little has been written about it and that few historians have used it to examine population levels or denominational composition in this mid-western part of Ireland in the 1740s. The census is extremely comprehensive and records the following information for each house:

- the names of the householder and spouse and adult kin, if any
- the religion of the above
- the occupation of the householder
- the total number of Protestant male and female children under 14 years of age
- the total number of Catholic male and female children under 14 years of age
- the total number of Protestant male and female children over 14 years of age
- the total number of Catholic male and female children over 14 years of age
- the total number of Protestant male and female servants
- the total number of Catholic male and female servants

The reason for Synge's instigation of this census is unknown and surprisingly he does not mention it in any of his writings or correspondence.[82] Neither is it known what inspired him to undertake the census in 1749, nine years after he succeeded to the bishopric.[83] The only clue as to the reason for the census appears in a letter written by Lord Edward Willes (1702–68), chief baron of the Irish court of exchequer, to his friend the earl of Warwick (Francis Greville) twelve years after the census was conducted in which he notes that 'The Bishop of Elphin has been very curious to know the proportion of Protestants to papists in his diocese'.[84]

   This census has a number of very important characteristics that makes it a very valuable source for understanding mid-eighteenth century rural Irish society. The religious denomination of married couples and their children is specified, thus allowing for the study of the degree and extent of interaction between the various religious communities including the number and proportion of marriages between members of different religions and the religion of their children. The clustering of Protestants in urban areas is also obvious from the data and the recording of occupations is particularly significant as it provides an insight into the variety of industries practised in the area at that time.

81 Census of the diocese of Elphin by religions, 1749 (N.A.I., M. 2466). The transcript in Roscommon county library, part typed, contains a number of inaccuracies, highlighting the importance of using original sources rather than copies where possible. **82** Synge's wrote over 200 letters to his daughter between 1746 and 1752 and in none of these did he mention the progress of the census, *The Synge letters*, ed. Marie-Louise Legg (Dublin, 1996) (hereinafter *Synge*, ed. Legg). **83** *Synge*, ed. Legg, p. x. **84** *The letters of Lord Chief Baron Edward Willes*, ed. Kelly, pp 1–17, 95.

It is unfortunate that the demographic inquiry initiated by Synge was not mirrored by other bishops throughout the country as the 1740s was a time of severe suffering and distress in the aftermath of the Great Frost of 1740–1.[85] Although all but written out of Irish history, the Great Frost, and the 1740s in general, marked a period of sharp if not unprecedented, distress.[86] Thereafter Charles Smith (1715–62), a member of the *Physico-Historical Society* and author of mid-eighteenth century county surveys for Cork, Kerry and Waterford, deduced from the reduction in the hearth-tax figures that the population of County Kerry had 'decreased nearly one third part, which was occasioned by the dreadful calamity of the great frost in 1739–40; and the great scarcity of the succeeding years of 1741, 1742, which were years of drought, death and sickness all over Ireland'.[87] In the baronies of Clondonagh, Upperwoods and Clarmallagh in County Laois, for example, the number of taxed hearths declined from an average of 2,285 per annum in the years 1736–40 to 2,032 (11 per cent) in the half-decade 1741–5.[88]

In the 1760s, by which time the country had largely recovered from the 1741 famine, the Irish House of Lords ordered that two more religious censuses be held. The first of these was conducted in 1764–5 and responsibility for gathering the data was again vested in the hearth-money collectors. None of the original data survives but copies for parts of the country may be found in various clerical succession lists and local histories.[89] Little examination of these figures has been carried out but as the hearth-money collector was the agent for recording the census, it can be presumed that the accuracy of the figures is questionable.

It was the manifest failure of this census that prompted the House of Lords to order the 1766 census,[90] instructing the various archbishops and bishops on 5 March,

85 Arthur Forde was appointed rector of Shankill parish in Counties Armagh and Down in 1748 and 'took a list of the Protestant and papish families for my own satisfaction'. This is the only census contemporary to the Elphin census and is not nearly as comprehensive, containing just population and family aggregates for Protestants and Catholics for each townland (N.A.I., M. 2476 (f)). A census of Cullen parish (south-west Tipperary) was conducted by the incumbent in the aftermath of this famine, to determine its true extent (David Dickson, *Arctic Ireland: the extraordinary story of the Great Frost and forgotten famine of 1740–41* (Belfast, 1997), pp 67–8). **86** For an introduction to the national impact of the 1740s famine see Dickson, *Arctic Ireland*. For a description of the impact of the 1740s on north-east Wicklow see Brian Gurrin, *A century of struggle in Delgany and Kilcoole. An exploration of the social implications of population change in north-east Wicklow, 1666–1779* (Dublin, 2000), pp 38–46, 60–68. **87** Charles Smith, *The ancient and present state of the county of Kerry*, p. 43. **88** Edward Ledwich, *A statistical account of the parish of Aghaboe in the Queen's County; Ireland* (Dublin, 1796), p. 47. **89** For example, 1764 and 1765 parish figures are available in Leslie, *Clogher*, p. 262 for various Monaghan and Fermanagh parishes. Comerford, *Kildare and Leighlin*, i, pp 269–70 and iii, p. 407 for some Laois, Kildare and Offaly parishes and Canon B. Troy (ed.), *Religious census of the diocese of Cloyne 1766 and other contemporary documents* (Midleton, 1998), pp 242–8. Also P.R.O.N.I., T.808/15261 for a number of parishes in Ulster, north Leinster and north Connaught. **90** Dickson, Ó Gráda and Daultrey, 'Hearth tax', p. 146.

to direct the parish ministers in their respective dioceses to return a list of the several families in their parishes to this House on the first Monday after the recess, distinguishing which are Protestants and which are papists and also a list of the several reputed Popish priests and friars residing in the parishes.[91]

As this census was to be organised by the bishops and the parish ministers, the parish and diocese was selected as the administrative basis of the inquiry.[92] Because principal responsibility for the inquiry lay with the parish incumbents, the accuracy of the returns was determined by each minister's enthusiasm for the exercise, his knowledge of his parish and his intimacy with his parishioners and the religious makeup of the parish. It has been argued that most ministers would have had a fairly good knowledge of their Protestant parishioners while estimates of the number of Catholics, though probably not as accurate, would nonetheless have been of the correct order.[93] Unsurprisingly, for parishes where both 1764 and 1766 figures survive, comparisons show the 1766 returns typically to report a higher population.

Like the originals of the hearth-tax rolls, most of the original 1766 census material was stored in the P.R.O. in the early twentieth century and was lost in 1922. It is fortunate, therefore, that at least a limited number of returns for many parishes had been transcribed by various copyists, including Tennison Groves, prior to their destruction. The only surviving original data is for various parishes in the dioceses of Armagh, Cashel and Emly, Cork and Ross and Waterford. A guide to the surviving returns and transcripts and their current location is available in the reading room of the National Archives.[94] The main stores for religious census manuscript materials are the N.A.I., the N.L.I., the R.C.B. Library and the P.R.O.N.I. In addition, significant amounts of the census data have been published over the years in various local journals and histories (see bibliography).

The quality of the returns and transcriptions varies enormously. As can be seen from the instructions issued to the parish ministers above, the returns were meant to include at a minimum the name of the householders, their religion and the names of any priests and friars ministering within their parishes. The best returns that are available are more detailed than this as they include the name and townland of each householder and also detail the denominational breakdown within each house. Such detailed returns exist for the Cork diocese parishes of Kilmichael and Carrignavar (known at the time as Dunbullock) for example. For other parishes, Protestant householders' houses have been similarly treated, as in the case of Edermine and Ballynaslaney in Wexford (these two returns also listing the religion of the household's servants) and Lurgan and

91 *I.H.L.J.*, iv, p. 370.   92 Dickson, Ó Gráda and Daultry, 'Hearth tax', p. 146. 93 'Parliamentary returns for the diocese of Raphoe, 1766', ed. T. O D. [Terence O Donnell?] in *Donegal Annual*, iii, no. 1 (1954–5), p. 74.   94 Religious census, 1766. A guide to surviving material (N.A.I., unpublished), p. 1.

Munterconnaught parishes in Cavan. A schedule of the returns that were available in the P.R.O. prior to its destruction is given in Wakefield's *Account of Ireland*, and if this is compared with the N.A.I. guide, the extent of the loss is readily apparent. Wakefield's schedule shows that Cork and Ross were the only dioceses to return the number of families and the number of people in every parish.[95]

From the available data it seems to have been quite common, particularly outside strongly Protestant areas, for Protestant householders' houses to contain Catholics as either family members or servants or both.[96] In Ballynaslaney parish, for example, the ten Protestant households were home to twenty-five Catholics between them while the fifty-eight Catholic homes housed no Protestants.[97] A little known (undated) return for Navan town also bears out this point.[98] The Revd Cyril C. Ellison, former rector of the Navan union of parishes and noted local historian, used the parish vestry book to date this return to 1761 rather than 1766 but even if this first date is correct, it is reasonably contemporary with the religious census.[99] In the return, 641 households were recorded as employing 244 servants. Sixty-nine of these servants were in the employ of Protestant householders, but only eighteen of the sixty-nine were Protestant while of the 175 servants in Catholic households only two were Protestant.

One factor that may have impacted on the quality of these 1766 returns was the short time span within which the returns were to be prepared and submitted to the clerk of the House of Lords, Henry Baker Sterne. Richard Stewart, minister of Louth parish, noted this in his return, stating that his return was made 'with as much care and exactness as the time would allow'.[100] Stewart's returns for Louth only contain Protestant and Catholic aggregates for each townland in his parish.[101] It seems probable that the parish tithe list was used by many ministers as the basis for their returns as it was a parish household-listing that most ministers would have had readily to hand.[102] The 1766 return for

95 Wakefield, *Account of Ireland*, ii, p. 587. Cork and Ross returns record 4,814 Protestant and 23,039 Papist families and 25,471 Protestant and 108,634 papist individuals giving an average household size of 4.81 for the two dioceses.   **96** For example see the return for Croagh parish, 'Protestant householders in the parishes of Croagh, Nantinan, Rathkeale and Kilscannell, Co. Limerick, in 1766' in *Irish ancestor*, ix, no. 2 (1977), pp 77–8. **97** N.A.I., M. 2476 (i). Also for the parish of Litter, County Cork, 'There are only 11 (eleven) Protestant families in this Parish, containing 77 persons who are of that Communion, and 31 persons besides, who are of the Popish Religion. There are 179 Popish families, among whom there is not a Protestant', Troy (ed.), *Cloyne*, pp 125–6. **98** Protestants of Navan (R.C.B., Meath Diocesan Archive, D7/12/2/1).   **99** C.C. Ellison, *Some aspects of Navan history* (Drogheda, 1964), p. 18 n. 24.   **100** 'The 1766 religious census for some County Louth parishes', ed. Tomás Ó Fiaich in *J.C.L.A.S.*, xiv, no. 2 (1958), p. 113.   **101** Ibid.   **102** 'The 1766 religious census for some County Tyrone parishes', ed. Tomás Ó Fiaich in *Seanchas Ardmhacha*, iv, no. 1 (1960–1), p. 147, L.P. Murray, 'The history of the Parish of Creggan in the 17th and 18th centuries' in *J.C.L.A.S.*, viii, no. 2 (1934), p. 127.

Termonfeckin parish, County Louth, notes that 'this list is taken by the Minister from the last return of the tithes of the parish ... [and consequently] it may not or cannot be perfect as one could wish ... considering the short warning'.[103]

Unfortunately, the parish tithe listing excluded the parish poor and thus any census based on a tithe list can be expected to underestimate the population to some degree. The Termonfeckin return, for instance, names nine Protestant and one hundred and sixty-one Catholic householders but casually notes that the list was deficient by 'forty or fifty poor cottiers and labourers who are all papists',[104] whereas other returns, by contrast, refer to them being 'exact' enumerations.[105] The comment regarding the incomplete nature of the tithe list that formed the basis for the Termonfeckin return is important as if this were typical of the extent of household-underestimation, then the 1766 religious census could only be viewed as a crude approximate that significantly underestimates the total population and in particular the number of Catholics. It must be said, however, that there is no evidence of the *universal* use of tithe lists in compiling returns, although it has often been presumed to have been the case that these tithe lists were used. However, it is unlikely that ministers would have wished to advertise the fact that their returns were based on such a list as this would have been seen by contemporaries as confirmation that their returns were deficient.[106]

The reason for the wide variance in the quality of the returns is suggested by Richard Lloyd, minister for Rathcormack, County Cork in the 1760s. He stated in his return that 'The order being general, and no particular method prescribed, I sent through the several plowlands of that Parish, and took the number in each'.[107] In table 9, examples of the variety in the quality of the returns are shown.

The diocesan summaries are particularly useful as they provide a clear picture of variations in denominational composition over a large area while also recording aggregate parish information that would otherwise have been lost. In respect of the Dublin diocese summary, for example, householder name-lists exist for no more than seven Dublin diocese parishes and unions whereas the Dublin summary contains parish aggregate information for more than twenty-five parishes. Furthermore, the information surviving in these summaries can be useful as in the case of certain parishes, the number of families and 'souls' (people) are recorded and these figures can be used as a guide to average family size.

---

103 'Louth' ed. Ó Fiaich, p. 117.   **104** Ibid.   **105** Comerford, *Collections*, i, p 271 for Monasterevan, Harristown and Ballybrackan; J.J. Fitzgerald, 'Notes on names of inhabitants of parish of Kilmichael in 1766' in *J.C.H.A.S.*, xxvi (1920), p. 73 for Killmichael.   **106** Tithe proctor assisted in compiling the Magourney and Killcolman, County Cork, returns. See Troy (ed.), *Cloyne*, p. 155.   **107** Ibid., p. 141.

Table 9. Examples of the variety in the quality of the 1766 census returns

Parish	Information in the return
Kilmichael, Carrignavar, both County Cork[108]	Head of family and number of Prots and RCs in each household only.
Lurgan & Munterconnaught, County Cavan.[109]	The Prot and Presbyterian house-holders listed and number of Prots and RCs in each household only.
Ballynure, County Antrim,[110] Ballynaslaney County Wexford.[111]	Ballynure, names of RC householders only. Ballynaslaney, names of Prot. householders only (also Prots and RCs within each listed household).
Rathdrum, County Wicklow,[112] Drumglass, County Tyrone,[113] Shankill, Counties Down & Armagh.[114]	Name of householder grouped by townland and religion indicated.
Marshalstown, Litter, both County Cork.[115]	Name of householder and number of males/females in each house.
Ardee union, County Louth.[116]	Only the name of the householder grouped by religion.
Louth, County Louth.[117]	Aggregate numbers of each religion per townland. No names recorded.
Union of Ballinderry and Tamlagh, County Tyrone,[118] Monaghan, County Monaghan.[119]	Aggregate numbers of each religion in the two parishes. No names or townland aggregates.
Diocese summaries[120]	Usually listing only the parishes in the diocese and the number of Prot and RC families in each.

108 J.J. Fitzgerald, 'Kilmichael', pp 69–73; 'Extracts from an old census', ed. An tOllamh Ó Donnchadha in *J.C.H.A.S.*, li (1946), pp 69–73. **109** 'The 1766 religious census, Kilmore and Ardagh', ed. Terence P. Cunningham in *Breifne*, i, no. 4 (1961), pp 361–2. **110** N.A.I., M. 2,476 (i) for Ballynure. **111** G.O. 537, p. 2. **112** G.O. 537, pp 112–24. **113** 'Tyrone', ed. Ó Fiaich, pp 149–50. **114** R.C.B., MS. 23, pp 6–16. **115** Troy (ed.), *Cloyne*, pp 101–4, 123–6. **116** 'A list of families around Ardee, 1766' in *J.C.L.A.S.*, x (1941–2), pp 72–6. **117** 'Louth', ed. Ó Fiaich, pp 112–13. **118** 'Tyrone', ed. Ó Fiaich, p. 57. **119** R.C.B., MS. 23, p. 21. **120** For example, Dublin diocese, N.A.I., M. 2,476 (i); Clogher diocese, R.C.B., MS. 23, pp 18–19; Kilmore and Ardagh dioceses, 'Kilmore and Ardagh' ed. Cunningham, pp 358–9.

PRE–CENSUS POPULATION SOURCES – ESTATE SURVEYS

Although all of the sources that have been examined so far originated from either Church or State inquiries and instructions, private individuals occasionally played a part in compiling population sources in pre-nineteenth century Ireland. In the main, private 'censuses' were conducted on a smaller scale than any of the enumerations considered thus far and typically their unit of study was the landlord's estate rather than the town, diocese, county or province.

The landlord's position in Irish society has been the subject of much historical scrutiny but few doubt that landlordism had an important influence on the Irish physical landscape. Kevin Whelan has observed that the third and last pronounced phase of urban development in Ireland was carried out under the supervision of landlords during the eighteenth century when many of the country's wealthier landlords, drawing on the fashions of England and continental Europe, laid out formal demesnes and naturalised parklands.[121] However, regardless of the size of an estate, each effectively operated as a business that required a steady income to meet the expenditure of the landlord and the costs of running his estate.

An estate's income was primarily sourced from the rent paid by its tenants. As rent levels were determined by the demand for land and the availability of money an estate's income was highly dependent on the population level (or the age structure of the population to be more accurate) and on the general economic climate at the time that the rents were set. It is important to remember that rents could be set for long periods and so the rental income of an estate was often determined less by the contemporary economic climate and population level than by rental agreements that were contingent on economic circumstances that had already passed. Cormac Ó Gráda notes, for instance, that the economic boom of the Napoleonic period (1793–1815) appears to have witnessed a steep rise in rents for new lettings that still had to be met by the tenant despite the onset of the post-war depression.[122]

Landed estates were such an intrinsic feature of Irish society down to the late nineteenth century that they were one of the four categories by which Hayes chose to group each county's sources in his *Manuscript sources*.[123] Such records can typically be found in three principal public locations, the N.L.I., the N.A.I. and the P.R.O.N.I., although some collections or parts of collections are also held in British repositories and in other overseas archives. Some estate records have remained in private hands and are consequently generally less accessible, but access will often be granted to genuinely interested parties. The best introductory guide to estate

121 Kevin Whelan, 'Towns and villages' in F. Aalen, Kevin Whelan and Matthew Stout (eds), *Atlas of the rural Irish landscape* (Cork, 1997), p. 180.   **122** Cormac Ó Gráda, *Ireland, A new economic history, 1780–1939* (Oxford, 1994), pp 28, 163–4.   **123** Hayes, *Manuscript sources*, vols vii, viii.

records, describing how to locate records and to interpret them, is Terence Dooley's *Sources for the history of landed estates in Ireland.*[124]

The most important estate records from a 'pre-census population sources' point-of-view are those that deal with planning, income and expenditure, as estate planning often required the surveying of the estate by professional surveyors. Since the purpose of these surveys was usually to provide the estate manager with up-to-date knowledge of his property so as to enable him to plan for the future, these surveys tended to include detailed maps, rentals and records relating to the planning of various estate improvements such as drainage and reclamation. Frequently, estate surveys were often conducted in the years before the termination of the estates' leases, in which case their purpose was principally to reassess the rent-potential of the estate. In the more sophisticated of these surveys, the population of the estate may be recorded. Accompanying estate maps can be of particular importance to the historian, depending, of course, on the quality and accuracy of their detail. Although the purpose of the estate maps can vary, the bulk of those produced tended to focus on showing the land divisions within the estate and the tenants who were in possession of same. The importance of estate maps in population studies is that they can pinpoint the location of houses in a townland and often distinguish between lands of differing quality. Thus estate maps, particularly if they are available for a number of different years, can show how the demographic makeup of an area varied over time. In addition, maps can be useful in determining the population on an estate by applying an appropriate multiplier to the total number of houses represented.

One of the best examples of an estate survey as a source for the study of a local population is that of the Fitzwilliam estate at Coolattin in south County Wicklow, carried out *c.*1730 and currently stored in the National Library of Ireland, as the survey is spatially extensive and yet presents a great deal of detailed population information.[125] Uniquely this is the only estate survey that Hayes chose to list in his *Manuscript sources* under the 'Population' heading.[126] The Fitzwilliam estate, covering one fifth of the total area of County Wicklow, was the largest in the county and was comprised of virtually all of the barony of Shillelagh, much of Ballinacor South, and small pockets of land to the north and east.[127] This survey focuses on that contiguous part of the estate centred on Coolattin.

It commences with a brief introduction concerning its purpose and there follows, among other data, a townland-by-townland record of the name of the immediate tenant, the names of the sub-tenants, the value of the rental, and an estimate of the potential market rent. The list of sub-tenants is particularly

124 Terence Dooley, *Sources for the history of landed estates in Ireland* (Dublin, 2000) (particularly pp 19–21). 125 Observations made upon the Rt Hon. The Lord Malton's estate in Ireland (N.L.I., MS. 6054). 126 Hayes, *Manuscript sources*, vi, p. 324. 127 William Nolan, 'Land and landscape in County Wicklow, *c.*1840' in Ken Hannigan and William Nolan (eds), *Wicklow: history and society* (Dublin, 1994), p. 657.

important as their names are often excluded from rental rolls. Each of the townlands and tenancies is briefly described and some of these descriptions can be both informative and prejudiced. Tinahely, for example, is described as being 'one of the poorest Towns in Ireland mostly inhabited by beggars, whores and rogues. It is impossible to put any valuation on that Town or farm. There is no trade in the Town and the land is Coarse & Barren'.[128] It is clear from the introduction to the survey and from the individual descriptions of the tenancies, however, that the surveyor holds the 'Romans' (Catholics) in contempt, necessitating careful consideration of his likely biases when using such descriptions.

From a demographic perspective this survey is quite exceptional in that it lists the religion (in many cases) and marital status of the tenants and the number of sons, daughters and servants they had. This provides direct evidence of the number of people per house in an extensive area of south Wicklow in the early eighteenth century. It was noted in the introduction to this guide that many of the pre-census population estimates used a household multiplier of between 5 and 6. However, the average household size from this estate survey is significantly lower at 4.49 per house[129] and is quite close to the contemporary figure of 4.36 that Dobbs reports for 'a great many contiguous Parishes in the County of Antrim'.[130] While one should be wary about some of the figures in the survey (certain townlands have very high numbers of two-person families raising suspicions that children may not have been rigorously enumerated in parts of the estate) it is, nonetheless, a fascinating early eighteenth-century source from which key demographic influences, principally the household-population multiplier, can be determined.

As established, the primary source of estate income was the rents paid by tenants. 'Rental rolls' recording the rent due from tenants and the actual rent that they paid to the estate can prove a fruitful population source for the demographic historian. If rental rolls exist for an estate for a prolonged period, changes in tenancy and rental levels, factors that were influenced by the demand for land, can be examined. These may also be used to determine periods of distress on the estate as one could reasonably expect arrears to increase during times of shortage although the link between distress and rentals is often too *inelastic* to be used for this purpose.

The most serious difficulty encountered in using rental rolls as a population source is that most only recorded an estate's immediate tenants and hence the number of tenants on a rental roll is unlikely to have equalled the number of households in the area. Some tenants may have sublet part of the land they leased from the estate and as the estate proper may have had little or no dealings with these sub-tenants, there would have been no consequent reason to record them

128 N.L.I., MS. 6054, p. 59.   **129** Dickson, Ó Gráda and Daultrey, 'Hearth tax', p. 151.
130 Dobbs, *Trade*, ii, p. 9.

Figure 3. Sample pages from Malton estate survey, County Wicklow, *c.*1730

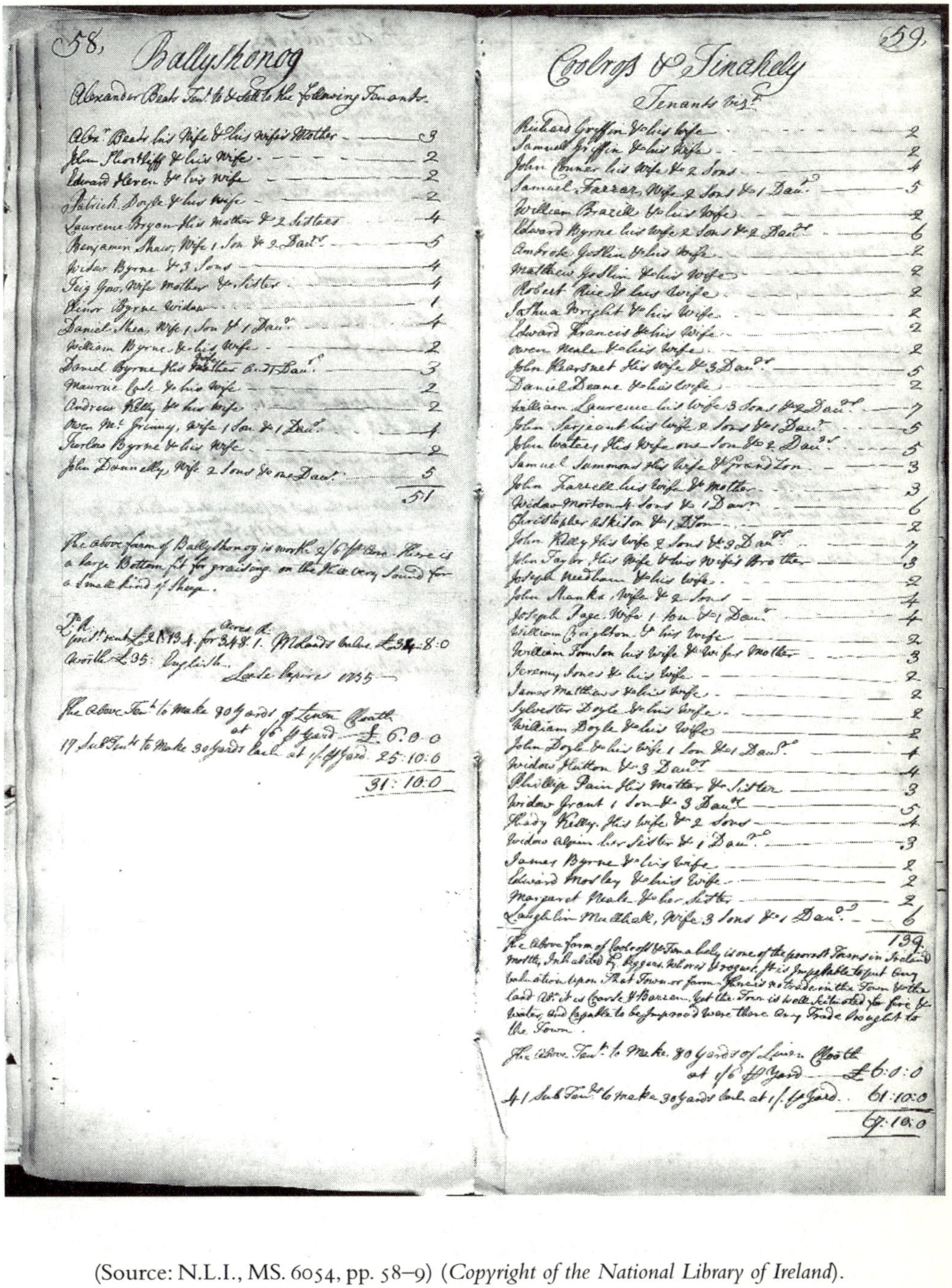

58, Ballyshonog

Alexander Beats Ten.t to & sett to the following Tenants

Alex.r Beats his Wife & his wifes Mother	3
John Shortliff & his Wife	2
Edward Heren & his Wife	2
Patrick Doyle & his Wife	2
Laurence Bryan his Mother & 2 Sisters	4
Benjamin Shaw, Wife 1 Son & 2 Dau.rs	5
Widow Byrne & 3 Sons	4
Teig Gow, Wife Mother & Sister	4
Elinor Byrne Widow	1
Daniel Shea, Wife 1 Son & 1 Dau.r	4
William Byrne & his Wife	2
Daniel Byrne his Wife and 1 Dau.r	3
Maurice Cole & his Wife	2
Andrew Kelly & his Wife	2
Owen Mc Grinny, Wife 1 Son & 1 Dau.r	4
Terlow Byrne & his Wife	2
John Donnelly, Wife 2 Sons & one Dau.r	5
	51

The above farm of Ballyshonog is worth 2/6 p.r Acre. There is a large Bottom fit for graising on the Hill very Sound for a Small kind of Sheep.

L. A. R. Acres R.
pres.t rent £21:13:4 for 348:1 Midlands value £34:8:0
worth £35: English.
Lease expires 1755

The above Ten.t to make 80 yards of Linen Cloath at 1/6 p.r Yard £6:0:0
17 Sub Ten.ts to make 30 yards each at 1/ p.r Yard 25:10:0
31:10:0

59, Coolross & Tinahely

Tenants viz.t

Richard Griffin & his Wife	2
Samuell Griffin & his Wife	2
John Conner his Wife & 2 Sons	4
Samuel Farrar, Wife 2 Sons & 1 Dau.r	5
William Brazill & his Wife	2
Edward Byrne his Wife 2 Sons & 2 Dau.rs	6
Ambrose Goslin & his Wife	2
Matthew Goslin & his Wife	2
Robert Rice & his Wife	2
Joshua Wright & his Wife	2
Edward Francis & his Wife	2
Owen Neale & his Wife	2
John Kearsnet His Wife & 3 Dau.rs	5
Daniel Doane & his Wife	2
William Laurence his Wife 3 Sons & 2 Dau.rs	7
John Serjeant his Wife 2 Sons & 1 Dau.r	5
John Waters His Wife one Son & 2 Dau.rs	5
Samuel Summons His Wife & Grand Son	3
John Farrell his Wife & Mother	3
Widow Morton 4 Sons & 1 Dau.r	6
Christopher Atkinson & 1 Son	2
John Kelly His Wife 2 Sons & 3 Dau.rs	7
John Taylor, His Wife & his Wife's Brother	3
Joseph Needham & his Wife	2
John Shanks, Wife & 2 Sons	4
Joseph Page, Wife 1 Son & 1 Dau.r	4
William Creighton & his Wife	2
William Fowlson his Wife & Wifes Mother	3
Jeremy Jones & his Wife	2
James Matthews & his Wife	2
Sylvester Doyle & his Wife	2
William Doyle & his Wife	2
John Doyle & his Wife 1 Son & 1 Dau.r	4
Widow Hutton & 3 Dau.rs	4
Phillip Pain His Mother & Sister	3
Widow Grant 1 Son & 3 Dau.rs	5
Shady Kelly, His Wife & 2 Sons	4
Widow Alpin her Sister & 1 Dau.r	3
James Byrne & his Wife	2
Edward Mosley & his Wife	2
Margaret Neale & her Sister	2
Laughlin Mullhall, Wife 3 Sons & 1 Dau.r	6
	139

The above farm of Coolross & Tinahely is one of the poorest Towns in Ireland mostly Inhabited by Beggars, Whores & rogues. It is Impossible to put any Valuation upon That Town or farm. There is no trade in the Town & the land &c. It is Coarse & Barran. Yet the Town is well Situated for fire & Water, and Capable to be Improved were there any Trade brought to the Town.

The above Ten.t to make 80 yards of Linen Cloath at 1/6 p.r Yard £6:0:0
41 Sub Ten.ts to make 30 yards each at 1/ p.r Yard 61:10:0
67:10:0

(Source: N.L.I., MS. 6054, pp. 58–9) (*Copyright of the National Library of Ireland*).

in the rental records. Fortunately estate expenditure records, usually recorded in *cash-books* and *day-books*, if available, can often be used to identify and enumerate sub-tenants. Unlike the rental rolls, which had little cause to record sub-tenants' names and activities, the latter are likely to appear in the cash-books on a regular basis. This is because although sub-tenants may not have been a direct source of income for the estate, they often presented themselves to the estate management when labour was required and any recompense for their services would consequently have been recorded. The estates' expenditure ledgers can present us with vital, if fleeting, glimpses of the otherwise unrecorded sub-tenantry. Unlike estate surveys which typically would have been expensive and irregular, the recording of expenditure in cash-books was usually made on a weekly basis at the very least. Thus, the cash-books can be used to provide a commentary on the fluidity of the sub-tenant layer of the social hierarchy within a given area by examining the names of those sub-tenants whose names recur year-on-year in the cash books as opposed to those tenants who drop out of the books altogether.

PRE-CENSUS POPULATION SOURCES — CHURCH RECORDS

The importance of church records as a fruitful source for the study of population trends in Britain has been clear since the founding of the Cambridge Group for the History of Population and Social Structure in 1964.[131] Although European censuses were pioneered by the Scandinavians in the eighteenth century, Britain did not conduct its first state census until 1801, with Ireland's first statutory census following twelve years later.[132] Nonetheless, various works based on an in-depth study of church registers by innovative demographers including Michael Drake, D.E.C. Eversley, Roger Schofield, E.A. Wrigley and J.H. Habakkuk have collectively shed valuable light on Britain's modern pre-census population history.[133]

---

131 'Introduction: local population studies' in Michael Drake (ed.), *Population studies from parish registers. A selection of readings from local population studies* (Derbyshire, 1982), p. xxvi, n. 2.   **132** Population statistics for some of the Scandinavian countries are far superior to those available for either Britain or Ireland. Iceland, for instance, held a census as early as 1703 for the purpose of determining the extent of poverty in the country. Later, censuses were held in that country in 1762, 1769 and 1782. Sweden introduced population estimates in the 1740s and national registration of population in 1748. The statistics produced by this Swedish system produced the 'outstanding demographic statistics of the eighteenth century'. Censuses were also hosted in Denmark in 1769 and 1787 and in Norway in 1769. See Glass, *Numbering the people*, pp 11–13.   **133** In the mid-eighteenth century a public debate had commenced in England concerning the population level of that country. A particular focus of this debate centred on whether the population of England and Wales had increased during the seven decades following the Glorious Revolution. Although much of the heat was taken out of the debate with the

Despite the relatively successful application of church record analysis in British population studies, Irish historians have been slow to follow the example of their British colleagues for a number of reasons. Firstly, the oldest parish records in Ireland belong to the Church of Ireland, which has always been a minority Church throughout most of Ireland outside of Ulster, the city and county of Dublin and its surrounds and some towns and pockets of territories which were once foci of English plantations. Even in the province of Ulster, for centuries the region in which Protestants were numerically most significant, the Church of Ireland community has historically been the third largest religious community, having fewer followers than both the Roman Catholic and Presbyterian Churches. Furthermore, unlike in England where records date back to the sixteenth century, Irish records are of more recent origin. In 1617 an attempt was made to require Church of Ireland ministers to keep registers and in 1634 it was written into the canons of the Church, but records for only five parishes predate 1650[134] and in 1672 Sir William Petty commented (not quite accurately) that 'Registers of Burials, Births and Marriages, are not yet kept in *Ireland*, though of late begun in *Dublin*, but imperfectly'.[135]

Obviously, for parish registers to be suitable for local population studies they must record the vital events (baptisms, marriages and burials) of a large section of the population of a local community. It is unsurprising, therefore, that much Irish demographic investigation has focussed on various areas in Ulster, where Protestantism has been strong since the seventeenth century and which boasts many of the oldest surviving parish registers. Some of the more significant demographic studies based on parish registers have been undertaken in the 1970s and 1980s by Valerie Morgan and William Macafee on parishes in Mid-Ulster, and laterally by Colin Thomas for Derry city and by William Macafee for County Tyrone. These studies will be considered in some detail in the following chapter where the usefulness of Protestant church records in population–change analysis in an area will become evident. Although Catholic records have been less widely used by historians, David Dickson's use of the registers for eight north-Leinster Catholic parishes in his study of mortality between the famines of the 1740s and the 1840s illustrates possibilities for drawing on these records for studying demographic trends in a local context.[136]

Prior to disestablishment (1871) the Church of Ireland registers, being the records of the state Church, were the property of the State. After disestablishment,

completion of a successful census of Britain in 1801, the debate proved to be so long lasting principally because English population statistics were inadequate, see Glass, *Numbering the people*, pp 11–40.   **134** *Register of the church of St Thomas, Lisnagarvey, Co. Antrim, 1637–1646*, ed. Raymond Refaussé (Dublin, 1996), p. 11.   **135** *The economic writings of Sir William Petty*, i, p. 210.   **136** David Dickson, 'The gap in famines: a useful myth' in E. Margaret Crawford (ed.), *Famine: the Irish experience, 900–1900* (Edinburgh, 1989), pp 102–3.

legislation was introduced to ensure that parish registers remained state property and thus, a great many Church of Ireland registers were stored in the P.R.O. and destroyed in 1922. Those wishing to use Church of Ireland records are advised first to consult Noel Reid's *A table of Church of Ireland parochial records and copies*, which lists the availability of Church of Ireland baptism, marriage and burial registers for all parishes in Ireland, their dates of commencement and also specifies which registers have been lost.[137] In many cases surviving records may be located in the R.C.B. Library or the P.R.O.N.I. The former began to receive parish records in 1939 and now holds the records of over 500 parishes. At the time of writing the library has launched a new appeal for records that remain in local storage in the various parishes to be deposited with the library for safekeeping. The library holds parish records from all over the country but particularly records from the Republic of Ireland. Records from Northern Ireland, when they are being surrendered by the local parish, are submitted to the P.R.O.N.I. rather than the R.C.B. Library as they cannot leave that jurisdiction.[138]

Unlike the Church of Ireland, which had a presence throughout the country, Presbyterianism was largely restricted to the north-eastern corner of Ireland. In 1861 96 per cent of Irish Presbyterians were resident in Ulster and 60 per cent were living in Counties Antrim and Down, the area of greatest Scottish settlement.[139] In addition, Presbyterian records rarely commence before the nineteenth century, even in Down and Antrim, and are therefore generally unsuitable for the study of pre-census population trends. Presbyterian registers for most of Northern Ireland are available on microfilm in the P.R.O.N.I. For an introduction to the development of the Presbyterian community in Ireland and to the available Presbyterian records see Christine Kinealy's essay in James G. Ryan's *Irish Church records*.[140]

Catholic records are also quite sparse before the nineteenth century, despite the fact that the majority of the population throughout most of Ireland professed allegiance to that Church. This is not surprising, however, considering the laws against popery which were in existence throughout much of the eighteenth century. The Catholic clergy were often poorly educated and semi-literate and many would have had difficulty in maintaining a register even if they had been so inclined. In addition, the anti-popery legislation, introduced in the aftermath of the Williamite victory, declared illegal the practice of Catholicism, banished priests from the two kingdoms from 1 May 1698 and required priests to be registered from 1704.[141] Unregistered priests caught ministering could be

137 Noel Reid, *A table of Church of Ireland parochial records and copies* (Naas, 1994). **138** Seamus Helferty and Raymond Refaussé, *Directory of Irish archives* (Dublin, 1999), p. 127; Raymond Refaussé, *Church of Ireland records* (Dublin, 2000), p. 14.   **139** W.E. Vaughan and A.J. Fitzpatrick, *Irish historical statistics: population 1821–1971* (Dublin, 1978), pp 52–3. **140** Christine Kinealy, 'Presbyterian Church records' in James G. Ryan (ed.), *Irish church records* (Salt Lake City, 1992), pp 69–105.   **141** James G. Ryan, 'Catholic Church records'

punished or put to death although the severity of the sanction varied from time to time and from place to place.

The penal legislation against non–Church of Ireland members (the Penal Laws also applied to Presbyterians)[142] was gradually relaxed from about the 1740s onwards but much of the legislation remained on the statute books and could be resurrected by a landlord, minister or magistrate if he so desired. As the threat of repression lessened and with the emergence of a Catholic middle class in the towns and cities as the eighteenth century progressed, it became less injurious to profess one's Catholicism and Catholic worship became more public as a result. Alongside these developments, and funded by a *nouveau riche* Catholic merchant class, the Catholic Church began to re-build its infrastructure and administration. The earliest Catholic parish records, primarily for city parishes, commenced in the 1730s. By contrast, in rural areas, which were for the most part devoid of a Catholic middle-class, the potential for the administrative and structural development of the Church was more limited.[143] There is a strong regional variation in the commencement of Catholic registers. Ryan has noted that 30 per cent of Leinster parish baptismal registers predate 1800. This contrasts with Munster where 11 per cent of extant registers predate the nineteenth century and Connaught and Ulster where the corresponding figure is only 3 per cent.[144]

For historical reasons the Catholic Church in Ireland does not have an administrative archive like the R.C.B. Library. Furthermore, unlike Church of Ireland records, Catholic registers are not 'public' records but are the property of the diocese to which the parish belongs and access to the records is controlled by the appropriate parish priest and bishop. Right of access to the registers, therefore, varies depending on the attitude of the particular bishop under whose jurisdiction they fall and the records for some dioceses are closed to the public. In the 1950s the National Library microfilmed the registers to ensure the survival of the information in the records but the bishops retain the copyright on these microfilmed copies. The original records are usually held in local custody and immediate access is controlled by the parish priest. However, since all parish records are available in the National Library on microfilm, requests for access to the originals will often be quite justifiably refused.

With the growth of interest in genealogical research in recent years the Irish Genealogical Project has commenced the indexing of parish records. These indexes are available in county heritage centres. While compiled to aid genealogical research in particular, they also provide the historian with a different perspective on a parish's registers and aid operations such as the enumeration of the recurrence of specific surnames.

in idem, *Irish church records*, p. 110.   **142** Kinealy, 'Presbyterian Church records', p. 70. **143** Ryan, 'Catholic Church records', p. 112.   **144** Ibid., p. 114.

MISCELLANEOUS SOURCES

In this chapter a variety of pre-census population sources have been introduced, their origins explained and their current availability briefly indicated. While an exhaustive list is impractical given the constraints of this guide, nonetheless it is hoped that the reader will now have a clear understanding of the origin, existence and usefulness of the more important pre-census sources for population study that are available to the local historian.

It may have been observed that some of the more popular genealogical sources have not been considered thus far. Sources such as subsidy-rolls, muster-rolls and poll lists (electoral-rolls) are typically listed in genealogy books as important sources for family history and yet they have not even been mentioned in this chapter. In point of fact, these sources have been deliberately omitted because, while they may be considered adequate as a genealogical resource, they do not fulfil the requirements of a population source. For a listing of names to qualify as a suitable population source, it must be comprehensive and representative of the entire population or of an entire community. These genealogical sources, however, are typically not sufficiently representative to be used as sources for estimating population levels.

Nonetheless, they do have certain uses in population studies. Of the afore-mentioned genealogical sources, subsidy rolls are by far the least representative of the general population as they record grants that were made to the Crown by the nobility, clergy and laity and are therefore strongly biased towards recording the wealthiest members of society. Surviving subsidy rolls, mostly dating from the 1630s and 1660s for some Ulster counties, can be consulted in P.R.O.N.I., the N.L.I. and the N.A.I. and can be located using Hayes' catalogue or a com-prehensive genealogical reference such as Grenham's *Tracing your Irish ancestors*.[145] A listing of surviving subsidy-roll data was published in *Analecta Hibernica* in 1982.[146] They can be used, however, for verification of data recorded in contemporary pre-census population sources such as the poll-tax summary or the hearth-tax rolls. A typical hearth-roll, for instance, should feature most if not all of the names listed in a subsidy roll dating from the same period. If it does not do so then this would suggest significant omissions from the hearth-roll as the latter should at least record the payments of the wealthiest people in society. In this fashion, Trevor Carleton has used a Tyrone subsidy-roll to examine the completeness of the 1660 poll-tax data for the 'four' Tyrone parishes for which the actual taxpayer name-lists survive. He notes that subsidy payers, Patrick Croly and Alex Wood, were recorded as mere labourers in the poll-tax list while James Hairs Esq. in the subsidy-roll was listed as a lowly James Harris Gent. in the poll-

---

145 Grenham, *Tracing your Irish ancestors*, pp 130–231.   **146** 'The subsidy roll of County Waterford', ed. Julian Walton in *Analecta Hibernica*, xxx (1982), pp 95–6.

tax list – a lower rank which would have saved him six shillings in tax.[147] Electoral poll lists are equally unrepresentative of the population because Roman Catholics were precluded from voting between 1727 and 1793.[148] As with subsidy-rolls, however, poll lists do have important, if limited, uses for the historian as they can be used to determine the extent and distribution of the Protestant population in an area.

Indeed many of the miscellaneous population sources are *Protestant-focussed* and will be of greatest use in estimating Protestant population levels. Muster-rolls, for instance, which record the number of men under arms that a principal landowner could 'muster' for military purposes, if required, are limited in this way. These rolls are available for much of Ulster for 1630 (see Grenham, *Tracing your Irish ancestors*) and typically, though not exclusively, list Protestant settlers willing to defend their settlements. For most parts of Ulster they are the earliest comprehensive listing of Protestants in an area. The 1630 muster-roll is available in the National Library and P.R.O.N.I.[149] In the next chapter the strengths and weaknesses of muster-rolls as sources for demographic research will be considered.

Against a background of renewed war between England and France, an 'agricultural' census of coastal areas was ordered in 1803 to determine the availability of livestock and 'dead stock' (foodstuffs and farm equipment). The purpose of the census was to ascertain what supplies would be available to the army in the event of a French invasion and what livestock and supplies would have to be removed from the coast if required. A secondary purpose was to determine the availability of manpower for yeomenry service.[150] The census was conducted by local constables and recorded the name of the householder (sons of householders are recorded in places) and the live and dead stock that he possessed. The surviving material, for fourteen parishes in County Antrim[151] and parts of County Down only, is available in the National Archives.[152] An index for the Antrim returns (7,338 names) is available on the reading room shelves in the National Archives.

Church of Ireland visitation records are similarly characterised by a strong Protestant bias. Occasionally during the seventeenth century, particularly when there were concerns about the state of the church in a diocese, bishops would 'visit' a diocese to conduct an inquiry into the state of Protestantism there. Typically the information recorded can include details of the physical condition of the church building, the average number of attendees at service, the value of tithes, the name of the church minister and so on. These detailed visitations often

147 Carleton, *Heads and hearths*, p. 176.　**148** Grenham, *Tracing your Irish ancestors*, pp 130–231.　**149** N.L.I., Microfilm 206.　**150** Paddy Walsh, 'Index to agricultural census, Co. Antrim 1803' (1993) (available in National Archives on reading room shelves). **151** Armoy, Ballintoy, Ballymoney, Ballyrashane, Ballywillin, Billy, Culfeightrin, Derrykeighan, Drumtullagh, Dunluce, Kilraghts, Loughguile, Ramoan, Rathlin. **152** N.A.I., OP 153/103.

contain comments concerning the strength of Protestantism or Catholicism in the parish but specific numbers are rarely given and in instances when numbers are provided, their accuracy can be questioned. Hayes' *Manuscript sources* lists the available visitation records and a number of these were published in early editions of *Archivium Hibernicum*.[153]

It can be useful to consult local histories or parish surveys when undertaking local demographic research as the recording of population information became popular at the beginning of the nineteenth century. William Shaw Mason's *Parochial survey* (microfilm copies are often available in county libraries) is worth checking as the typical parish entry contains contemporary (*c.*1814–9) population estimates while many parishes contain earlier data.[154] The sections that demographic historians will be primarily interested in when using the *Parochial survey* are sections III ('Modern Buildings, &c.') and V ('Present & Former State of Population, Food, Fuel, &c.'). The appendix entry for the parish should also be consulted as very detailed figures can be presented here. Other general sources such as the Dublin Society's *Statistical Surveys* (covering eighteen counties although only the Antrim volume contains particularly detailed population data), the earlier Physico-Historical Society statistical accounts of Waterford, Kerry, Cork and Down and Edward Wakefield's *Account of Ireland* should also be considered.[155]

Local censuses were occasionally conducted by enthusiastic individuals for philanthropic or personal-interest reasons – the celebrated 1798 census of Dublin being a case in point.[156] James Whitelaw, vicar of St Catherine's parish in Dublin, organised this census which 'amounting to nearly five hundred tables in folio'[157] recorded for each house:

• the name and occupation of the householder
• the number of upper and middle class males and females
• the number of male and female servants
• the number of lower class males and females
• the state of repair of the house
• the number of stories

---

153 'Visitatio regalis, 1615. Cashel and Emly', ed. Michael Murphy in *Arch. Hib.*, i (1912), pp 282–311; 'The royal visitation of Cork, Cloyne, Ross, and the College of Youghal', ed. idem in *Arch. Hib.*, ii (1913), pp 173–215; 'The royal visitation, 1615. Diocese of Killaloe', ed. idem in *Arch. Hib.*, iii (1914), pp 210–26; 'The royal visitation, 1615. Dioceses of Ardfert [and Aghadoe]', ed. idem in *Arch. Hib.*, iv (1915), pp 178–98; 'Royal visitation of Dublin, 1615', ed. Myles V. Ronan in *Arch. Hib.*, viii (1941), pp 1–55; 'Archbishop Bulkeley's visitation of Dublin, 1630', ed. idem in *Arch. Hib.*, viii (1941), pp 56–98. **154** Mason, *A statistical account or parochial survey of Ireland*. Seventy-nine parishes and parish-unions are covered in the three volumes.   **155** Wakefield, *Account of Ireland,* ii, pp 497–727.   **156** James Whitelaw, *An essay on the population of Dublin being the result of an actual survey taken in 1798* (Dublin, 1805).   **157** Ibid., p. 5, advertisement.

Unfortunately, financial limitations made the publication of the entire census impossible and it was 1805 before it was published in summary form. The manuscript census was stored in the P.R.O. and was destroyed in 1922. The summary data includes details of the number of houses and the number of males and females resident on each street in the city's nineteen parishes and a summary table presents the social breakdown of each parish.[158]

In short, there is a wealth of pre-census population data available and it remains the job of the individual local historian to source the population data that are available for his or her locality and to make an informed assessment as to the completeness or otherwise of those sources. In the next chapter some consideration will be given to the matter of how one should best use these population sources.

---

158 Ibid., pp 14–15.

CHAPTER 3

Researching pre-census demographic sources: some problems and possibilities

It has been shown that some parts of the country have a wider array of pre-census population sources available than do others and that Leinster and in particular Ulster have the broadest range of sources available while data is most limited for Connaught. Consider the hearth-tax data for instance. Hearth-rolls are available for part or all of eight of the nine Ulster counties and four of the twelve Leinster counties[1] for various years during the 1660s (see appendix B). By contrast, hearth roles are only available for Tipperary in Munster and Sligo and Galway City (1724) in Connaught. Not surprisingly, therefore, the majority of seventeenth and eighteenth-century demographic analysis has focussed on locations in Ulster and Leinster.

The aim of this chapter is to show researchers how best to use those sources that are available and to point to tests that should be applied to them to determine their suitability as bases for population studies. Problems that may be encountered in using the sources will be highlighted and a number of published population studies will be introduced to show how professional historians have interpreted various sources and presented their analyses. Statistical analysis of the data in population sources is an unavoidable feature of population studies and the reader will therefore be introduced to some basic statistical analysis in the course of this chapter.

The most important thing to remember when using pre-census population sources of any form is that population sources, like all historical records, are inherently biased and are almost certainly deficient to some degree. The onus is then on the historian to endeavour to ascertain what the biases in the sources may be and how these may have influenced the accuracy and integrity of the data contained therein. Once this is done, an educated guess can then be made as to how the data should be adjusted to take account of suspected omissions. If no attempt is made to adjust the figures to account for suspected biases, then any conclusions based on the raw data will be compromised.

Consider the case of a taxation-roll, for instance – one of the more common types of pre-census population sources. It is a common exercise to analyse first names and surnames in taxation-rolls to try to determine the religious

1 Mullingar and Kildare hearth data are not included.

breakdown of the population in an area. However, such an analysis is problematic, as it is quite possible that one or other confessional group may have paid a relatively higher proportion of tax by virtue of their greater wealth or their typical settlement patterns and will consequently be over-represented in the roll. It is also probable that tax was less assiduously collected in thinly-populated areas, thus depressing the relative importance of such areas in the roll. If the opportunity for fraud in the tax collection process existed – which was usually the case – then the probability that the roll is deficient as a result of unscrupulousness must also be considered. Biases such as these are inherent in every source and the historian is best advised to approach a source with a healthy scepticism regarding its accuracy, rather than slavishly accepting its data as correct.

A MULTIPLICITY OF MULTIPLIERS

It will have been noted that few of the sources described in the previous chapter are actually censuses as that term is understood today. This is hardly surprising, however, as a census is a costly exercise requiring detailed planning, scheduling and supervision and obviously the more data collected, the higher the cost of conducting the census and analysing the results. Although it has been argued earlier that one's primary focus in a demographic study should not be on producing population estimates but rather on looking for trends and comparing relative population sizes, the generation of population estimates remains a worthwhile exercise which may provide baseline figures that can be used, for instance, in the determination of 'snapshot' birth and death rates. Thus, if a researcher is dealing with a source such as a taxation return or a religious census that focussed on counting families as opposed to individuals, a multiplier can be used to convert the recorded data to 'population-estimate' data.

The majority of the population sources discussed thus far have been taxation returns of one form or another. Unfortunately, however, taxation-based returns are not the ideal basis on which to determine the magnitude of population in an area at a particular time. This is because taxes, by their nature, are an outgoing which most would wish to avoid paying if at all possible. If loopholes exist in tax legislation exempting people from the tax, these will be found and exploited. If the loopholes are not closed off, with the passage of time the proportion of the public avoiding paying the tax will obviously increase. For example, it seems incontestable that the hearth-tax rolls preceding the 1665 amending legislation are, in general, less representative of the total population than are the post-amendment rolls, which are themselves imperfect.

The vernacular settlement pattern of rural areas must also be considered when trying to determine the degree of omission from rolls. Traditional Gaelic settlements in the form of *clachans* were still commonplace throughout Ireland in the seventeenth century and, like the urban context, these clusters would have facilitated the hearth-collector whereas the typical rural Protestant settlement pattern of scattered homesteads would have been less amenable to universal taxation. Regardless of the type of settlement pattern in an area, it is unlikely that Catholics would be significantly over-represented in a universal taxation-roll such as a hearth-roll. However, it is possible that in areas where the rundale system of agriculture was prevalent, Catholic under-representation was less pronounced than may have been the case in urban areas.[2]

For hearth-rolls dating from the 1660s, in most cases one can compare the rolls with the 1660 poll-tax data to see if deficiencies in either of the sources can be identified. Specifically, one should try to detect areas or individual townlands that have been omitted from one or other of the sources. Hearth-tax and poll-tax data can also be compared with *Civil survey* material if it exists for the area under study, again for the purposes of identifying whether taxation data for specific areas are missing.[3] If one wishes to compare data in the hearth-tax with that in the poll-tax an immediate difficulty arises, however, as the rules governing hearth-tax payments and poll-tax payments differed substantially. Most obviously, the hearth-tax was a charge on a household and each name recorded in a hearth-tax roll represents one household, regardless of the number of persons living in that house or the age structure of the occupants. By contrast, the poll-tax was, at least in theory, imposed on all adults in a household including women, adult children and servants. Thus, to make a valid comparison between hearth-tax and poll-tax figures for a particular area, one must apply appropriate multipliers to both sets of figures to convert the data to population estimates.

To illustrate this point, appropriate multipliers for the hearth- and poll-tax figures for Drangan parish, County Tipperary are suggested below. The hearth and poll figures for this parish are shown in Table 10 and are illustrative of a number of points that were made earlier concerning the widening of the tax burden following the 1665 hearth-tax amendment.

When comparing data from various types of sources one should be conscious that the same administrative boundaries may not apply between the sources. This problem is evident in Table 10 as the 1665–6 data covered only Drangan parish, the 1666–7 hearth figures included two townlands from Magowry parish and the 1660 poll-tax figures incorporated an additional townland from St Johnstown parish and three townlands from Cooleagh parish (Kilbreedy, Lismortagh and Meateestowne). Thus, in Table 10 the 'Adjusted parish total' row only includes Drangan townlands whilst the 'Total numbers listed' incorporates

2 I am grateful to Professor Kerby Miller for help with this point.   3 *The Civil Survey: A.D. 1654–6*, ed. Robert C. Simington (10 vols, Dublin, 1934–61). Counties covered include Tipperary (vols i and ii), Donegal, Derry and Tyrone (vol. iii), Limerick and pt Kerry (vol. iv), Meath (vol. v), Waterford (vol. vi), Dublin (vol. vii), Kildare (vol. viii), Wexford (vol. ix), miscellaneous volume with part of Louth (vol. x).

Table 10. Hearth- and poll-tax figures for Drangan parish, County Tipperary

	1665–6 Hearth-tax		1666–7 Hearth-tax		1660 Poll-tax		
	Houses	Hearths	Houses	Hearths	English	Irish	Total
Drangan	8	8	25	27	0	61	61
Priesttown	4	4	13	13	0	36	36
Newtown	8	8	13	13	4	42	46
Clonihea	2	2	9	9	3	6	9
Corbally	5	5	0	0	0	28	28
Ballynenane	10	10	22	22	2	29	31
Magowry			13	13	3	40	43
Ballylosky			9	9	0	12	12
St. Johnstown				0	4	83	87
Kilbreedy				0	0	10	10
Lismortagh				0	0	25	25
Meateestowne				0	0	40	40
Total numbers listed	37	37	104	106	16	412	428
Adjusted parish total	37	37	82	84	9	202	211

all figures, including those extraneous to the parish proper. In cases such as this, one could easily be deceived into assuming that the poll-tax reported in greater detail than did the hearth-tax rolls.

When generating a population estimate from a taxation-roll the first task is to try to estimate the extent of exemptions from the roll. Only when this is done should a multiplier be applied to the adjusted figures to convert the taxation data (usually the total number of houses or taxpayers) to a population estimate. In the case of hearth-tax data, William Macafee has applied correction factors of 2 for 'Planter' (English) and 4 for Irish families to the 1666 Tyrone hearth-roll (preceding the implementation of the 1665 amending act), on the grounds that Irish (Catholic) families were less likely to be taxed than Protestants.[4] If these correction figures are accepted for pre-amendment hearth-rolls (and they are no more than an educated guess) then suitable correction factors for post-amendment rolls (principally Antrim, Tipperary and Wicklow), based on the information in Table 7, would be of the order of 0.25 for Protestant and 2 for Catholic families.

4 William Macafee, 'The population of County Tyrone, 1600–1991' in Charles Dillon and Henry A. Jefferies (eds), *Tyrone: history and society* (Dublin, 2000), pp 457–8.

Once the housing figures have been adjusted to take account of exemptions and omissions, a suitable multiplier, in this case representing the average household size, can be applied for the purpose of generating a population estimate. Obviously the average number of persons per house in an area will have fluctuated, perhaps significantly, over time and will have been influenced by such factors as customs and traditions, the rent price of land, the economic state of the area, the degree of urbanisation and so on. Most of the pre-census population estimates presumed the average household size to be between 4.5 and 6 persons. This is quite a significant variation, however, as a population figure based on the higher figure will be 33 per cent greater than an estimate that presumed the average household size to be 4.5. Dickson *et al* have produced a table showing a variety of multipliers for various parts of the country between 1684 and 1800.[5]

The listed multipliers range from a suspiciously low 3.90 for Armagh city (this is very low for an urban setting) in 1770 to a figure of 7.67 for an admittedly small sample size in Limerick city in 1684, with most of the multipliers for the period 1684–1800 falling into the 4.5–5.25 range. There is a noticeable increase in the multiplier size after 1779, which may be accounted for by population pressures reducing the availability of land and thus increasing the average age of marriage or forcing married couples to live in the family homestead after marriage.

It should also be noted that average household size could vary quite significantly within a very small area. In the 1766 census returns for the Delgany union in north-east Wicklow, for example, the average household size for Protestant household varied between 4.5 per house in Delgany parish and 5.57 per house in the neighbouring parish of Kilmacanoge whereas the figure for Catholic households varied between 4.6 in Kilcoole parish and 5.14 in Delgany. Throughout most of the country, with the exception of Ulster, Protestant households were typically larger than Catholic households, this difference being accentuated by Protestants' greater tendency to keep servants. However, as already stated in the previous chapter, in Protestant households the servants were often Catholics and it was more common for a Protestant householder to have a Catholic spouse than *vice versa*. Thus the total Protestant population in an area was usually less than the total number of people living in Protestant households whereas the Catholic population typically exceeded the total number of people in Catholic households.

One must also consider that households were generally larger in urban areas. Sir William Petty recognised this as early as the 1680s when he used a multiplier of 6 for multi-hearth houses, which were predominantly located in urban areas, as compared with a multiplier of 5 for the 'poor Cabineer families'.[6] The much-criticised 1706 population estimate, discussed in the first chapter, provided a slightly more detailed set of multipliers, presuming there to be 5 persons per

5 Dickson, Ó Gráda and Daultry, 'Hearth tax', p. 151.   6 *The economic writings of Sir William Petty*, ii, p. 606.

single-hearth and 7 persons per multi-hearth rural house and 4.5 persons per single-hearth and 8.5 persons per multi-hearth house in Dublin.[7] Arthur Dobbs later noted that the average number of persons per house in two (unnamed) Dublin city parishes and two (unnamed) suburban parishes was $12\frac{1}{12}$ and that one house contained 70 persons.[8] It is clear, therefore, that unless there are specific average household-size figures available for an area, any chosen multiplier can be at best viewed as an educated guess, although few would fault the use of a multiplier in the 4.5–5.5 range for rural areas and a multiplier in the 5.5–6.0 range for urban areas (in Dublin in the eighteenth century average household size was in the 10-12 range). However, one must be remember that the derived result is an *approximation* rather than an *accurate population estimate*. A multiplier for converting the 1660 poll-tax return to a population estimate is a little more difficult to derive as an accurate multiplier would be influenced by the age-profile of the population of the area in question. Furthermore, there is some doubt as to the degree of omissions and exemptions from this tax and even contemporaries recognised that some people who were obliged to pay the tax had managed to avoid it. In the poll-money ordinance of 1661 a fascinating portrait of tax evasion is presented as it was noted that

> the insolvencies and deficiencies of the two former Polls [the 1660 return was the first of these] hath principally risen from, and been occasioned by the removal of many of the Under-tennants, and meaner sort of people out of the Towns and Villages wherein they did inhabit at the time of making up the Estreats, or Lists of the Inhabitants of such towns and Villages'.[9]

In addition, Carleton has argued that the rolls for the four Tyrone parishes for which *actual* poll-tax rolls survive[10] strongly indicate that children of taxpayers aged fifteen or upwards may have evaded the tax on a massive scale and that about 50 per cent of the householders paying the hearth tax in 1664 in these four parishes had managed to evade the poll-tax three years earlier.[11] Although this 'exemption' rate may be accurate for the four parishes in question, it is certainly an overestimate for the country as a whole.[12] Indeed it is interesting that

---

7 T.C.D. MS. 833, ii, p. 330.   **8** Dobbs, *Trade*, ii, p. 10.   **9** *Census Ire.*, *1659*, p. 637. **10** Poll-tax rolls exist for Aghaloo, Donaghedy, Urney and Termonmaguirk parishes. The Aghaloo and Termonmaguirk poll-lists are for the second poll-tax, which presumably fell due in the second half of 1660.   **11** Carleton, *Heads and hearths*, p. 177.   **12** If we accept that the 1664 hearth tax roll was deficient by approximately 70 per cent (Macafee, 'Tyrone', p. 457), then only about 15 per cent of householders paid the poll tax according to Carleton. Carleton also suggested massive evasion on the part of children of fifteen years plus. The poll tax would thus enumerate perhaps 20 per cent of the total number liable for the tax. If this rate were to hold for the entire island then Hardings estimate for the population would increase from 0.5 million to 2.5 million. However, Hardinge did not realise that the 'census' was in fact a poll tax and that the 2.5 million payers would equate to about 5 million people!

Tyrone is one of the five counties for which no taxation returns exist in the poll-tax summary and there is evidence to suggest that the returns for these five counties were so obviously incomplete or deficient that they were never even compiled.[13]

L.M. Cullen has applied a multiplier of 3 in converting the poll-tax to a population estimate, basing this figure on William Hardinge's crude readjustment to take account of the missing counties in the return and his own readjustment of Sir William Petty's 1672 hearth-tax figure.[14] William Smyth has assumed a multiplier of 2.5 for areas where the returns are considered to be reliable, although as already stated, he does council that it is wiser to avoid working with absolute totals and to concentrate instead on inter-baronial comparisons.[15] It is this author's opinion that Cullen's multiplier is probably the more suitable figure for a number of reasons. Firstly, Petty implied a multiplier of the order of 2.4 for converting figures for the total number of adults (16 years of age upwards) in 1672 to a national population estimate. Secondly, although far removed in time from the poll-tax return, an analysis by the author of the *c.*8,000 people enumerated in Crosserlough parish, County Cavan, in the 1821 census shows an average household size of 5.35, which approximates to the typical multiplier used with hearth-tax data. The multiplier for factoring people of sixteen years of age and over into the calculation of the total population, however, was only 1.73 and even if servants are excluded, the multiplier rose to just 2.05.[16]

Table 11. Summary details for Crosserlough parish, County Cavan

Houses	Uninhabited	Total Inhabited	Pop.	Avg. age	>15	Servants etc.	Pender's multiplier I.e. > 15.	Pender's multiplier > 15 (excl. servants)	Hearth-roll multiplier
1474	38	1436	7882	22.69	4543	693	1.73	2.05	5.35

(Calculated from: *Crosserlough, County Cavan 1821 census*, ed. Marie Keogh.)

13 See 'An estimate of the pole money', T.C.D., MS. 808, f. 275, where no poll-money estimates are listed for Cavan, Mayo and Tyrone, three of the five counties for which no returns exist in the poll-tax summary. The other two counties missing from the poll tax are Galway and Wicklow. For Galway there are poll-tax estimates for Galway county but not for Galway 'towne'. In 1672 the Wicklow hearth-tax farm revenue was ranked tenth in Leinster, being 50 per cent larger than Longford's and 30 per cent larger than Carlow's. For the poll-money estimate, however, the Wicklow estimate is the smallest in Leinster, being 25 per cent less than Carlow's and 13 per cent less than Longford's. Note also that Hardinge, 'Earliest known manuscript census', p. 325, estimated the omitted figure for Wicklow at 6,066, greater than the Carlow and Longford figures. **14** L.M. Cullen, 'Population trends in seventeenth-century Ireland', pp 152–3. **15** Smyth, 'Society and settlement', p. 56. **16** *The economic writing of Sir William Petty*, i, pp 144–5; *Crosserlough, Co. Cavan 1821 census*, ed. Marie Keogh, Irish genealogical sources, no. 17 (Dublin, 2000).

Thirdly, from John South's estimate of the population of Dublin in 1696[17] men and women, exclusive of servants, accounted for 54 per cent of the population. Even if it is conservatively assumed that only one third of the 17 per cent of the population who were servants were adults, then South's estimate reported that adults comprised 60 per cent of the total population of the city, thus requiring a multiplier of 1.7 to convert an enumeration of adults in Dublin to a total population figure for the city.

With these examples suggesting multipliers of less than 2.4 to convert adults to population estimates, if an allowance is made for those legally meeting the tax exemption qualifications and also for people who had managed to avoid the tax (the adult children suggested by Carleton, for instance), a multiplier of 3 would appear to be of the right order. In Table 12, guide adjustment factors and multipliers for pre- and post-amendment hearth-rolls and for the 1660 poll-tax are shown.

Table 12. Adjustment factors and multipliers for pre- and post-amendment hearth-rolls and for 1660 poll-tax

Source	Adjustment factor	Multiplier
Pre-amendment hearth roll	2 for Protestants, 4 for Catholics.	4.5–5.5 (rural), 5.5–6.0 (urban) 10–12 (Dublin).
Post-amendment hearth roll	0.25 for Protestants, 2 for Catholics.	4.5–5.5 (rural), 5.5–6.0 (urban).
1660 poll-tax		3 (including adjusting for exemptions)

If we apply these adjustment figures to the Drangan parish figures in Table 10, adjusted population estimate figures (based on an average household size of 5) can be produced. These adjusted population estimates (Drangan parish townlands only) are shown in Table 13. In generating these figures it was presumed that it was not necessary to apply 'the Protestant adjustment factor' for the hearth rolls as the parish was predominantly Catholic. As can be seen, the 1666–7 post-amendment hearth-tax based population estimate of 820 is 30 per cent greater than the poll-tax based estimate. A population increase of this magnitude is unlikely to have occurred in the short period between the poll-tax and the hearth return. Nonetheless, all three population estimates are of the same

17 T.C.D., MS. 883, i, p. 83, 'An exact account of ye number of houses, hearths & people in Dublin in ye 10th January 1695/6'.

order and, as noted earlier, one's focus should not be so much on the actual population estimate as on population *trends* and *relative* sizes. Furthermore, deficiencies of this order could be a result of the tax collectors assuming different parish or townland boundaries thus showing the essential need to always consider surrounding areas when studying a specific area.

Table 13. Adjusted population estimates for Drangan parish, County Tipperary

Townland	Hearth-tax 1665–6			Hearth-tax 1666–7			Poll tax 1660			
	Houses	Adj. houses	Pop. est.	Houses	Adj. houses	Pop. est.	English	Irish	Total	Pop. est.
Drangan	8	32	160	25	50	250	0	6	161	183
Priesttown	4	16	80	13	26	130	0	36	36	108
Newtown	8	32	160	13	26	130	4	42	46	138
Clonihea	2	8	40	9	18	90	3	6	9	27
Corbally	5	20	100	0	0	0	0	28	28	84
Ballynenane	10	40	200	22	44	220	2	29	31	93
Total	**37**	**148**	**740**	**82**	**164**	**820**	**9**	**202**	**211**	**633**

A key feature of the poll-tax summary is that it shows not only the number of taxpayers in townlands within a parish, but also the number of English and Irish taxpayers.[18] It is usually presumed that the proportion of English and Irish taxpayers in an area mirrors the Protestant/Catholic religious division in the region. While this is not strictly accurate, the ethnic split can be viewed as a fair guide to the religious breakdown in an area in the mid-seventeenth century (except for Antrim, Down and east Derry where Gaelic-speaking Scottish Protestants were recorded as 'Irish'). As already noted with the hearth-money rolls, however, it is likely that 'Irish' were less likely to pay the tax and consequently the English (Protestant) proportion may be exaggerated.

In the previous chapter, two Protestant-specific sources were introduced, Ulster muster-rolls dating primarily from the 1630s and the 1740 Protestant householders lists. By virtue of their being largely, though not exclusively, Protestant-orientated, these rolls can at best be used to estimate the number of Protestants in an area and, unless the religious balance is known, they cannot be used effectively as a guide to the total population. Robert Hunter has used them to study the development of early Protestant settlement in Cavan and Donegal.[19]

18 Scottish taxpayers are enumerated with the English in all Ulster counties except Monaghan and most of Antrim. The only places outside Ulster for which Scottish payers are recorded is Agha parish, County Tipperary and St Johnstown, County Longford. 19 'The Muster Roll of *c.*1630: Co. Cavan', ed. R.J. Hunter and M. Perceval-Maxwell in

The rolls are not household-based but being lists of potential fighting men, they recorded healthy men of fighting age – presumably those in the 16–45 years of age bracket. Unlike taxation-based records, exemptions on the basis of poverty would be minimal, so muster-rolls would represent a broad spectrum of the adult male Protestant community. Writing in the early nineteenth century, Edward Wakefield noted that a number of contemporary writers suggested that about 25 per cent of a community were capable of bearing arms.[20] While allowing for the fact that some males will have avoided being registered, a multiplier of the order of 6 would seem appropriate for converting the total number of names in a muster-roll into a total population estimate for the Protestant population. However, the rolls for each county or area vary in terms of completeness and in those cases when there is evidence of serious omissions, a greater multiplier would be required.[21]

The 1740 Protestant-householders lists, unlike the muster-rolls, are household-based. This is surprising because, like the muster-rolls, they were compiled because of the need to arrange for the organising of a militia so one could expect them to enumerate males of fighting age. It would appear that the lists only include Church of Ireland householders but this may vary from place to place and, where possible, the surnames listed should be compared with those appearing in the near-contemporary 1766 census returns. In the absence of any alternative data such as estate rentals, Church of Ireland parish registers or 1766 census returns, one is safest assuming a multiplier of 5 – representing the average number of persons per family – to convert the householders list into a Protestant population estimate.

From this discussion concerning the use of multipliers the difficulties in using non-census sources to generate population estimates are self-evident. One is on somewhat surer ground, therefore, when dealing with actual censuses rather than taxation- or military-based sources as, by definition, a census should be more comprehensive. In the previous chapter a number of 'religious' censuses conducted between the 1730s and the 1760s were identified. The first of these, stemming from official concerns over the continued growth of popery in the early decades of the eighteenth century, coincided with a 1731 *Inquiry into the state of Popery*. While little of the 1731 census has survived[22] the contemporary popery inquiry, although

Breifne, v, no. 18 (1977–8), pp 206–22; R.J. Hunter, 'The settler population of an Ulster plantation county' in *Donegal Annual*, x, no. 2 (1972), pp 124–54.   **20** Wakefield, *Account of Ireland*, ii, p. 693 where Morton Pitt, Malthus and Price all suggest that one quarter of a population can bear arms. Other examples provided by Wakefield, however, suggest that the ratio of the total population to the number on the militia rolls could be as high as 12:1 – Wakefield provided the following figures in *An account of Ireland*; in Waterford city 3,199 out of 40,000 (8 per cent) on city militia roll, p. 709; Annakill parish, County Down, 318 out of 2,100 (15 per cent) liable to serve on militia, p. 704; Belfast, 'only one-eight of the population of the town' (12.5 per cent), p. 693.   **21** Hunter, 'The settler population', p. 126, considers the roll for Cavan to be quite complete and notes the same for Londonderry (T.W. Moody, *Londonderry plantation* (Belfast, 1939), pp 278–9, 319–22) but considers Armagh to be 'conservative'.   **22** See Tighe, *Statistical observations relative to*

containing no population level data,[23] contains important information such as the number of priests, friars, 'Mass houses' (including the numbers built since George I's accession in 1714), popish schools and the instances of local conferences between Protestants and Catholics on a parish basis. Indeed, despite its failure to record population figures, one can infer from the numbers of schools and houses recorded, as Patrick Fagan has done in the case of Dublin city parishes, the relative size of the Catholic population of various parishes.[24] In fact, it is likely that this assumption would be more suitable in the case of rural parishes than it was for Fagan's analysis, as inhabitants would have had less distance to travel to attend schools in neighbouring parishes in an urban environment.

The educational information recorded in the inquiry is particularly interesting and although there is little data concerning the quality of the education, the presence of schools in most parishes suggests the possibility that a basic education was provided for a small number of Catholic children. The teaching of English to Catholic children was common. In the school in Kilcock, County Kildare, for instance, 'one Patrick Ryly, a Popish schoolmaster, teacheth young children English'[25] and in Cloyne diocese 'the poorer sort of Irish Natives making no scruple to send their Children, to learn the English Tongue in the Protestant schools'.[26]

The apparent lack of contact between the Protestant minister and his Catholic equivalent is also striking and in the majority of cases, the names of the Catholic priests (or even the number of priests) in the parish were unknown to the minister. Despite this lack of contact, however, the report notes that several of the Mass houses seem to have been built since 1714. Whether this is a reflection of an easing in the enforcement of legislation against Catholics in the years before the report was compiled or simply an indication of the flimsiness of Catholic buildings at the time requires further study.

The religious censuses of the eighteenth century were primarily organised for the purpose of determining the strength of Catholicism in the country. Consequently the actual data recorded was very specific and the surviving data varies greatly in terms of coverage, quality and reliability. The Lords' instructions for the 1766 census, for example, requested ministers to make returns detailing the number of families in their parishes but ministers varied in their degree of adherence to these instructions. Therefore, in places for which family numbers

County Kilkenny, pp 453–63 and Leslie, *Ossory clergy and parishes*, pp 184–372. **23** Occasionally population information was provided in the returns. The ratio of Catholics to Protestants in Mayo was estimated at a minimum 12:1 (*I.H.L.J.*, iii (1727–54), p. 169. Kill parish had a population of 80 Protestants and 800 Papists in 1729 (Comerford, *Kildare and Leighlin*, i, p. 265). The population of Cloyne diocese was also estimated (*Arch. Hib.*, ii (1913), p. 128). **24** Fagan, 'The population of Dublin in the eighteenth century', pp 135–6.   **25** Comerford, *Kildare and Leighlin*, i, p. 263.   **26** 'State of Popery' in *Arch. Hib.*, ii, p. 128.

are available, a multiplier can be used to estimate the total population. As with the hearth-tax figures, this multiplier would be of the order of 4.5–6.0 (higher for urban Dublin), depending on whether the area was urban or rural. Where diligent ministers made complete census returns incorporating householders' names a number of further possibilities for study are opened up to researchers. Comparisons between surnames as they appear in religious censuses, hearth-rolls or Griffith's Valuation can provide a useful indication of the degree of continuity or change in land-holding patterns in an area.[27] Analysis of surnames in religious censuses can also be used as an aid to estimating the denominational breakdown in an area from sources such as taxation rolls, which do not contain any information concerning religious denominations.[28] Uniquely, and in contrast to these national religious censuses, the 1749 religious census of the diocese of Elphin, recorded a wealth of information regarding the population structure, the employment of servants and the distribution of the various types of employment in the diocese in the mid-eighteenth century at a time when the region was recovering from the disastrous famine of 1741.

VERIFYING CENSUS DATA

Thus far in this chapter it has been shown how some of the various censuses and census substitutes may be interpreted to recreate 'snapshot' population estimates. The discussion concerning the use of multipliers and adjustment factors should have made the fruitlessness of trying to estimate accurately the population level from pre-census population sources evident, as the suggested multipliers and adjustment factors are, at best, only guideline figures. Consequently it has been advised that a demographic study of a locality should also consider the population history of surrounding areas so that their relative population sizes can be compared. Moreover, it is useful to compare pre-census population estimates with the early statutory census data as one can usually have more confidence in the accuracy of the nineteenth-century data[29] which is available decennially for the whole island from 1821.[30] Religious breakdown data is available for 1831, 1834 and decennially from 1861.[31]

In reality, however, the generation of 'population snapshots' is often not of any great historical interest as they are likely to tell us very little about the intricacies

---

27 See William Macafee, 'The colonisation of the Maghera region of South Derry during the seventeenth and eighteenth centuries' in *Ulster Folklife*, xxi (1977), pp 70–91, for example.   **28** See Cormac Ó Gráda, 'Liam or Jason? What's in a name?' in *History Ireland*, vii, no. 2 (1999), pp 38–41 for a rare example of first name analysis.   **29** See Gurrin, *Delgany*, and Kennedy, Miller and Graham, 'The long retreat', pp 31–61 for examples of this approach.   **30** Vaughan and Fitzpatrick, *Population 1821–1971*, pp 355–67 for census references from 1821.   **31** *First report of the commissioners of public instruction, Ireland*, H.C.

of life and of the periodic demographic rhythms experienced by the people of an area. In order to advance one's analysis beyond the superficial aggregates and number sequences determined from these various enumerations, one must draw upon other sources, the primary focus of which was the recording of specific social and economic interactions. As already noted, two of the most important of these 'social' sources are church and estate records and if the researcher is fortunate enough to have these records available, the possibilities for creating a more complete population picture are greatly enhanced. However, the quantity and quality of the social and demographic information that can be extracted from estate or church records is determined by two factors – the extent to which the records are representative of the general population of the locality and the completeness of the records themselves.

It is difficult to undertake all but the most rudimentary analysis of such records without first computerising the data. The most appropriate tool for storing data in electronic format is a spreadsheet package and although data-entry is a time-consuming task, the benefits of having the data available in a spreadsheet are great. Typically spreadsheets support filtering and sorting of data and various statistical operations can be performed quickly and easily.

A good policy to adopt when entering data in a spreadsheet is to enter the data in the format recorded in the source and then to reduce the data to its lowest common denominators and enter this information as separate data. This makes it particularly easy to perform operations on whatever specific infor-mation one wishes to work with. For instance, when dealing with dates, it is useful to record the date in one spreadsheet cell but also to record in three separate cells the day, month and year for that date. This facilitates the sorting and filtering of the data by month or by year, which is not as straightforward a task if only the date is recorded. For convenience, it is a good idea also to enter dates in 'American format' (that is year/month/day) instead of Irish format (day/month/year) and always to enter months and days as two-digit entries (that is 02 for February or 09 for the ninth day of the month and so on) as this supports the sorting of entries by date, in ascending or descending order. Dates prior to 1752 (old-style – new year commenced on 25 March, each year) should also be converted to the new-style date format. When dealing with money or land-area values, researchers should similarly enter the data as it appears in the source and in a separate cell enter the equivalent decimal value. For instance, 1 acre, 2 roods and 4 perches is equivalent to 1.55 acres, and so on. Examples of entering date and monetary values are shown in Tables 14 and 15. It should be noted that all spreadsheets support the writing of *formulae*, which can parse date, area or money data, thus automatically generating many of these entries.

Table 14. Entering date data in a spreadsheet

Date as in source (day/mth/yr)	New date (yr/mth/day)	Year	Month	Day	Day of week
20/02/1697	1698/02/20	1698	Feb	20	Sun

Table 15. Entering monetary values in a spreadsheet

Money value (£:s:d)	Money value (£)
10:5:6	10·27

In the previous chapter it was shown that day-books and cash-books, effectively the petty cash books and wages records of the estate, can provide details of the sub-tenants, casual labourers and cottiers that would not otherwise have been recorded. In addition, these records can be used to identify years of distress and can indicate the type of agriculture practised in an area, a factor which was an important influence on the periodic rhythms of an agricultural society.[32] While rental-rolls are usually poor sources for estimating population levels, there is a wealth of socio-economic demographic related information that can be garnered from them. One of the most interesting areas of examination concerns the rental value per acre information available uniquely in the rental-rolls. While farm-size information or rental value per acre data are not ideal indicators by themselves of population pressures, one can safely conclude that evidence of small farms with high rental values is indicative of a large population and vice versa. By comparing changes in farm sizes and rents per acre over a period of time on an estate, the researcher can endeavour to verify the static population level data that may be available from the various census-type sources already considered. Griffith's Valuation and the Ordnance Survey name-books provide a mid-nineteenth century reference point with which any results can be compared.

Church records, by contrast, contain completely different but no less important material and if one has suitable (that is representative and largely complete) parish registers at one's disposal, a whole new avenue of analysis is opened up as exemplified in the very readable *Population studies from parish registers* edited by Michael Drake and the more detailed *The population history of England 1541–1871: a reconstruction* by E.A.Wrigley and R.S. Schofield.[33] That there have been no

1835 [45], xxxiii. **32** Ann Kussmaul, *A general view of the rural economy of England, 1538–1840* (Cambridge, 1990), pp 14–45. **33** Michael Drake (ed.), *Population studies from parish registers* (Derbyshire, 1982); E.A.Wrigley and R. S. Schofield, *The population history of England, 1541–1871: a reconstruction* (Cambridge, 1989).

books published on this topic in Ireland is itself indicative of the relatively primitive state of Irish demographic analysis.

The most basic forms of analysis that can be carried out on parish registers are the graphing (bar graphs are the most appropriate) of yearly aggregates for vital events (baptisms and burials in particular), with the burial graph being particularly useful for identifying periods of distress. Those unfamiliar with basic statistical analysis should consult an introductory guide such as *Teach yourself statistics* by Alan Graham or *Statistics without tears* by David Rowntree.[34] It is also useful to graph the aggregated baptisms minus the aggregated burials on an annual basis as such a plot will clearly show the years of natural population increase (when baptisms exceeded burials) and decrease, and those years featuring very high numbers of burials or baptisms will be immediately evident. However, if the yearly fluctuations are pronounced and the data is plotted over a long time period, an annual plot of baptisms, marriages and burials can appear cluttered. In such cases the burial and baptism data should be aggregated over a period longer than a year, so as to observe the general natural population trends. Typically a ten-year period is chosen, as it is sufficiently long to mask the large fluctuations that may be manifest when examining annual data.

Bar graphs such as these are useful in verifying the snapshot population data that may be obtained from pre-census population sources. If the snapshot data suggests that the population has changed substantially between two periods, then this change should be manifest in the baptism and burial plots as an increased population will usually be reflected in a higher number of baptisms and burials and *vice versa*. In general, one should expect to see roughly 30–50 baptisms, 20–30 burials and 8–15 marriages per annum for every 1,000 persons.[35]

Having compiled annual and decennial-aggregate graphs of the number of vital events relating to a local population, the first task to be undertaken is the identification of burial and baptismal peaks and troughs. A burial peak is particularly significant as it is likely to denote a period of extreme distress in the area, although one should be aware that the peak could be caused by other, less dramatic reasons (the parish minister or the graveyard in the parish or in a neighbouring parish may be temporarily unavailable, for instance). Years in which the burial level exceeds the baptism level should be identified, as this is suggestive of a natural population decrease. If burials exceed baptisms for a number of successive years, this can be an indication of prolonged distress resulting in an actual decline in the population.[36] Baptism fluctuations can also be indicative of

34 Alan Graham, *Teach yourself statistics* (London, 1999), pp 47–64; Derek Rowntree, *Statistics without tears: an introduction for non-mathematicians* (London, 2000), pp 38–48. **35** See D.E.C. Eversley, 'A survey of population in an area of Worcestershire from 1660 to 1850 on the basis of parish registers' in D.V. Glass and D.E.C. Eversley (eds), *Population in history: essays in historical demography* (London, 1965), p. 404 for some sample figures for twelve Worcestershire parishes.   **36** Gurrin, *Delgany*, pp 33–40 for examples of this

contemporary economic conditions – David Dickson noted that burial peaks were often followed within a year by a fall in the baptism level[37] whilst an increase in baptisms is typically an indicator of improving socio-economic conditions resulting in increased fertility.

If snapshot population-level estimates are available for a number of years, it is possible to estimate the crude birth and death rates (per 1,000 people) for these years. It should be borne in mind that baptisms and burials do not equate directly to births and deaths and that different ministers may have followed different methods of registration. However, birth (baptism) and death (burial) rates are the most convenient method of comparing varying baptism and burial levels for periods with different population levels.

Two of the more common statistical operations performed on a data set are the determination of mean and mode values for the data set. Researchers unfamiliar with these terms should reference the relevant section in a basic statistics reference such as Graham's *Teach yourself statistics*.[38] The mean of a set of values is the sum of the values divided by the number of values while the mode is the most frequently occurring number in the set of values. One must be careful how the results of these analyses are interpreted, however, as the results from statistical operations can sometimes prove misleading. Specifically, one should be aware when calculating the mean of a set of values that extreme values can grossly skew results and render them meaningless. Consider the case where the researcher is trying to determine the birth-baptism interval and is working with a data set comprising nine children who were baptised after seven days and one child who was baptised after two years (730 days). Statistically, the mean for this data set is 79.3 days, a figure that is completely misleading and actually disguises the true birth-baptism interval. In cases where a small number of values in a data set can grossly skew the true result, these values should be excluded from the calculation of the mean. Thus, the actual mean for the data set given above is seven days (calculated from the nine homogeneous values) with one child baptised after two years.[39]

The basic statistics and simple graphs described above can provide a wealth of demographic information not available from other pre-census source materials. Valerie Morgan, for instance, used annual baptisms, marriages and burials aggregates and decadal averages to pinpoint periods of population increase or decline in her demographic studies of the parishes of Blaris (Lisburn), Coleraine and Magherafelt published in the 1970s.[40] Using this simple methodology she was able to construct

approach. **37** Dickson, 'The gap in famines: a useful myth?', pp 102–3. **38** Alan Graham, *Teach yourself statistics* (London, 1999) pp 65–87. **39** Ibid., pp 104–8. **40** Valerie Morgan, 'A case study of population change over two centuries: Blaris, Lisburn 1661–1848' in *Irish Economic and Social History*, iii (1976), pp 5–16; idem, 'The Church of Ireland registers of St Patrick's, Coleraine as a source for the study of a local pre-famine population' in *Ulster Folklife*, xix (1973), pp 56–67; idem, 'Mortality in Magherafelt, County

a credible analysis of population change in these diverse areas. In the case of Blaris parish, despite the 'unavailability' of an accurate base population figure'[41] the general demographic trends occurring between 1661–1848 were identified and those years for which the burial level was particularly high were noted.

When studying Magherafelt, Morgan had wished to use the parish registers to draw a comparison with the findings from her earlier study of Coleraine but was unable to do so because of variations in the different incumbents' methods of recording.[42] As in the case of Blaris, in the Magherafelt study Morgan calculated average figures for baptisms, marriages and burials in an effort to trace the contours of population change between 1717 and 1736. She hypothesised that that an excess of burials over baptisms during the 1720s and 1730s suggested that the Church of Ireland population was in decline at this time.[43] Mean, median and mode values for the interval between births (baptisms) were also estimated, which matched figures from other pre-industrial societies in England.[44]

Also during the mid-1970s William Macafee published a study of the Maghera, south Derry, region in the seventeenth and eighteenth centuries.[45] Unlike Morgan's studies, which relied exclusively on parish registers, Macafee's work on Maghera was a more detailed analysis of population change in the region which drew on a wide variety of sources other than parish records to produce a more rounded study of colonisation and social development in the area. In the early 1980s Macafee and Morgan jointly produced two further important demographic studies, a reappraisal of eighteenth-century mortality in Magherafelt in the early eighteenth century using the Magherafelt Church of Ireland registers,[46] and a general work on population change in Ulster between 1660 and 1760.[47] The Magherafelt study is particularly important because it uses census-substitute sources such as the Derry hearth-roll of 1663, the 1740 Protestant household return and the 1766 religious census return in conjunction with the Church of Ireland registers. Using 1766 census material, Morgan and Macafee were crucially able to distinguish sub-groups of people who were using the Church for registration.[48] One such group was the Dissenter community, which was using the registers for burials but not for baptisms. Thus, the excess of burials over baptisms recorded in the registers during the 1720s and 1730s, which Morgan had interpreted as indicative of distress among the Church of Ireland community, was actually not a manifestation of a falling Church of Ireland population during this

Derry, in the early eighteenth century' in *I.H.S.*, xix, no. 74 (1974), pp 125–35.   **41** Morgan, 'Blaris', p. 7.   **42** Morgan, 'Mortality in Magherafelt', p. 126.   **43** Ibid., p. 128.   **44** Ibid., p. 129.   **45** Macafee, 'The colonisation of the Maghera region of South Derry', pp 70–91.   **46** William Macafee and Valerie Morgan, 'Historical revision xxi: mortality in Magherafelt, County Derry, in the early eighteenth century reappraised' in *I.H.S.*, xxiii (1983), pp 50–60.   **47** William Macafee and Valerie Morgan, 'Population in Ulster, 1660–1760' in Peter Roebuck (ed.), *Plantation to partition* (Belfast, 1981), pp 46–63. **48** Macafee and Morgan, 'Magherafelt' pp 51–2.

period.[49] Rather that community's population was increasing at the time. However, the presence of non-Church of Ireland names in the burial register but not in the baptism register gave the appearance of a natural population decrease among the Church of Ireland community.[50]

Thereafter, there was little of consequence published in the field of Irish demographic studies until 1985 when William Smyth's essay entitled 'Property, patronage and population' was published in *Tipperary: history and society*.[51] Smyth's essay is a masterful portrayal of changing human geography in mid-seventeenth century County Tipperary, making use of the *Civil survey* data for that county to construct a view of the 'proprietorial' make-up of the county in 1640, against which the 1660's poll-tax and hearth-tax data was compared. More recently, Colin Thomas has published a study on population change in Derry city between 1650–1900 in *Derry/Londonderry: history and society*[52] and an examination of family formation in Derry city, 1650–1750.[53] Thomas' two essays represent the first significant demographic inquiry undertaken in Ireland that has focussed on a large urban setting. William Macafee has also examined population change in County Tyrone from 1600 in *Tyrone: history and society*.[54]

Having ascertained the general population trends and identified periods of distress or prosperity for a local population, the seasonal 'rhythms' manifest in the registers can then be studied. Researchers may find the investigation of linkages between the timing of baptisms and marriages and the type of agricultural practised in the area a fruitful course of examination. In a famous study, Ann Kussmaul, following on the earlier work of Wrigley and Schofield, studied marriage seasonality in a number of parishes in pre-industrial England. She found that the agricultural and industrial make-up of the parish was a significant determining factor for the timing of marriages. The seasonal demand for labour in arable areas differed greatly from the labour demand in pastoral areas. In arable areas the demand for labour peaked during the spring when the ground was prepared and the seeds sown and again in late autumn when the crops ripened. The autumn harvest period was particularly critical and during harvest time the demand for labour was often so great as to require day labourers from nearby towns to satisfy that demand. Typically rates of pay increased to a yearly maximum during the harvest, in arable areas. Pastoral areas, by contrast, required

49 Morgan, 'Mortality in Magherafelt', p. 128.   **50** Macafee and Morgan, 'Magherafelt', pp 51–3.   **51** William Smyth, 'Property, patronage and population – reconstructing the human geography of mid-seventeenth century County Tipperary' in W. Nolan (ed.), *Tipperary: history and society* (Dublin, 1985), pp 104–38.   **52** Colin Thomas, 'The city of Londonderry: demographic trends and socio-economic characteristics, 1650–1900' in Gerard O'Brien (ed.), *Derry/Londonderry: history and society* (Dublin, 1988).   **53** Colin Thomas, 'Family formation in a colonial city: Londonderry 1650–1750' in *Proceedings of the Royal Irish Academy*, 100 C, no. 2 (2000), pp 87–111.   **54** Macafee, 'The population of

greatest labour expenditure during the late winter and in springtime when lambs and calves were born and required weaning.

Kussmaul found that because of the variation in the timing of the demand-peak for labour in arable and pastoral areas, these areas displayed fundamentally different patterns in terms of marriage seasonality. In arable areas, marriages peaked in late spring and early summer when labour was plentiful. Marriage was comparatively rare, however, during the autumn when demand for labour was at its highest. She explains this trend by arguing that labourers could not afford to forego the opportunity of earning higher wages during the busy season, nor could they expect their acquaintances to do so, for the purpose of celebrating a marriage. It was more sensible to earn the higher wage at harvest time and celebrate when work was scarcer and wages were lower.[55] The seasonal rhythms were less marked in pastoral areas and as part-time work was less widely available in such areas, marriage seasonality tended to be less manifest.[56] Kussmaul also found that marriages were often crammed into the holiday periods around Easter (marriages were discouraged during Lent) and Christmas and argued that this trend can be explained in similar terms, with no wages foregone if marriage was held during the holiday period.

This author has studied the seasonality of marriage in the vicinity of Delgany and Kilcoole, County Wicklow, a predominantly arable area, in the eighteenth century and has found similar patterns to those reported by Kussmaul.[57] It was further observed that baptisms dipped during the harvest period, a trend also related to the agricultural makeup of the area. As female physical labour was critical to the successful harvesting of the crops, the opportunity cost of not having a woman's labour available at this time was high. Thus, it was argued that the dip in baptisms during the autumn and the absence of a peak in the aftermath of the harvest, was a result of necessary family planning and birth control.[58]

Church records uniquely allow the historian to explore the rhythm of family life. Numerous variables that had a direct bearing on the rate of population change of an area can be determined only from an examination of church records. One of the most important influences on the fertility rate was the average marriage age of females. The lower the average age of marriage, the higher the potential fertility rate and usually the higher the actual fertility rate and *vice versa*. Unfortunately, in pre-nineteenth century parish registers the age of the bride is rarely recorded, which renders determination of the marriage age problematic. In the absence of a specified marriage age for brides, the only way of determining the average age at marriage is by examining the baptism registers to see if a record of the brides' baptism can be located. Unless specific local conditions dictated otherwise (periodic absence of clergy, for instance), it is

County Tyrone, 1600–1991'.   **55** Kussmaul, *A general view of the rural economy of England*, p. 17.   **56** Ibid., p. 22.   **57** Gurrin, *Delgany*, pp 53–6.   **58** Ibid., pp 41–3.

usually safe to presume that baptism closely followed the birth of a child and so the baptism–marriage interval can be presumed to differ little from the birth–marriage interval.[59] As brides were required by law to be at least sixteen years of age, the success of this 'count-back' process is dependent on the marriage and baptism registers being relatively complete over a period of a quarter of a century or so. Although many researchers will be reluctant to undertake this laborious task, the rewards in the form of detailed and specific marriage-age information makes the exercise worthwhile.[60] Tracking fluctuations in the average age of marriage can be used to gauge general population trends discerned from data contained in other sources.

Other population-influencing variables that can be determined from parish registers include the 'marriage-first birth' intervals and the number of baptisms per family. The latter is especially important, particularly if it can be observed over a period of time, as this figure is directly related to the average family size, which has already been afforded consideration when discussing how house numbers can be translated into population estimates.

59 See Ronald W. Herlan, 'Age at baptism in the London parish of St. Olave, Old Jewry, 1645–1667' in Drake, *Population studies from parish registers*, pp 55–61; Donald M. McCallum, 'Age at baptism: further evidence' in ibid., pp 62–4; Ian G. Doolittle, 'Age at baptism: further evidence' in ibid., pp 65–8. Taking an Irish example, in the case of Delgany Church of Ireland parish (County Wicklow), reliable birth-baptism interval information does not become available until 1819. Of the 290 baptisms between 3 October 1819 and 29 October 1826 for which a birth-baptism interval is known the months with the largest average intervals are August (20.5 days), November (19.9 days), March (17.6 days) and December (16.2 days). Evidence from England shows that the birth-baptism interval increased in the late eighteenth century and if this was also the case in Ireland the birth-baptism interval can be presumed to be almost contemporaneous. **60** Gurrin, *Delgany*, pp 48–51.

Conclusion

The potential for conducting demographic inquiry into pre-nineteenth century Ireland was severely restricted when, on 30 June 1922, the Four Courts, home to the Public Records Office, was destroyed. Although the possibilities for demographic research were irreparably impaired by this tragic loss, enthusiastic researchers have succeeded, particularly over the past thirty years, in extracting a great deal of demographic information from the surviving source material in pursuit of demographic-trend reconstruction. Undoubtedly the opportunities for population studies are more limited in Ireland than in other European countries. However, if one is prepared to invest time in demographic analysis the results can be surprisingly fruitful. It is hoped that this pamphlet has helped readers by identifying key sources and suggesting possible areas of inquiry in the field of demography in pre-nineteenth century Ireland.

Appendices

APPENDIX A. HEARTH-MONEY COUNTY FARM TOTALS

See Dickson, Ó Gráda and Daultry, 'Hearth-tax', p. 179 for a more complete list of hearth-money farm totals. The figures below are those available in T.C.D. MS. 883.

Table 16. County farm total for hearth-tax

Counties	Years					Percentage change in years			
	1672	1682	1683	1684	1685	1672–82	1682–83	1683–84	1684–85
L'derry	705	880	887	897	900	24.82	0.80	1.13	0.33
Donegal	605	880	913	914	941	45.45	3.75	0.11	2.95
Antrim	1,353	1,620	1,662	1,712	1,737	19.73	2.59	3.01	1.46
Tyrone	563	868	879	879	907	54.17	1.27	0.00	3.19
Down	1,105	1,365	1,408	1,458	1,481	23.53	3.15	3.55	1.58
Monaghan	355	379	402	424	474	6.76	6.07	5.47	11.79
Armagh	517	567	574	621	671	9.67	1.23	8.19	8.05
Cavan	460	609	643	654	634	32.39	5.58	1.71	−3.06
Fermanagh	350	444	478	489	445	26.86	7.66	2.30	−9.00
Ulster	**6,013**	**7,612**	**7,846**	**8,058**	**8,190**	26.59	3.07	2.70	1.64
Leitrim	288	352	360	364	370	22.22	2.27	1.11	1.65
Sligo	415	590	608	615	615	42.17	3.05	1.15	0.00
Mayo	520	700	710	746	760	34.62	1.43	5.07	1.88
Galway	1,349	1,466	1,550	1,580	1,590	8.67	5.73	1.94	0.63
Roscommon	615	735	805	820	825	19.51	9.52	1.86	0.61
Connaught	**3,187**	**3,893**	**4,033**	**4,125**	**4,160**	22.15	3.60	2.28	0.85
Louth	580	613	635	638	679.4	5.69	3.59	0.47	6.33
Meath	1,217	1,275	1,296	1,330	1,330	4.77	1.65	2.62	0.00
Longford	305	400	410	420	420	31.15	2.50	2.44	0.00
Westmeath	[620]	747	762	762	762	20.48	2.01	0.00	0.00
Dublin City	1,620	2,365	2,380	2,974.6	2,973.8	45.99	0.63	24.98	−0.03
Dublin County	610	608	600	750	725	−0.33	−1.32	25.00	−3.33
Wicklow	457	570	580	600	610	24.73	1.75	3.45	1.67
Kildare	640	775	810	820	820	21.09	4.52	1.23	0.00
King's County	530	645	650	640	600	21.70	0.78	−1.54	−6.25
Queen's County	600	605	650	665	665	0.83	7.44	2.31	0.00
Carlow	345	370	370	375	382	7.25	0.00	1.35	1.87
Kilkenny	890	1020	1021	1051	1000	14.61	0.10	2.94	−4.85
Wexford	891.5	920	920	942	955	3.20	0.00	2.39	1.38
Leinster	**9,305.5**	**10,910**	**11,084**	**11,967.6**	**11,922.2**	14.78	1.59	7.97	−0.38
Clare	605	755	780	810	820	24.79	3.31	3.85	1.23
Limerick	1,020	1,365	1,410	1,410	1,403	33.82	3.30	0.00	−0.50
Waterford	673	785	796	815	818	16.64	1.40	2.39	0.37
Tipperary	1,298	1,506	1,529	1,563	1,572	16.02	1.53	2.22	0.58
Cork	2,760	3,365	3,338	3,375	3,402	21.92	−0.80	1.11	0.80
Kerry	600	850	830	830	800	41.67	−2.35	0.00	−3.61
Munster	**6,956**	**8,626**	**8,683**	**8,803**	**8,815**	24.01	0.66	1.38	0.14
Yearly total	25,461.5	31,041	31,646.6	32,953	33,087.2	21.91	1.95	4.13	0.41

(Source T.C.D., MS. 883.i, p.73)

APPENDIX B. AVAILABLE HEARTH-TAX ROLLS AND SUMMARIES

Hearth-tax manuscript material can be located using Hayes' *Manuscript sources*, MacLysaght's listing in *Analecta Hibernica* and Carleton's list in *Heads and hearths*.[1] The table below lists published hearth-tax rolls and hearth-tax figures and manuscript materials that have been omitted from the above references.

Table 17. Available hearth-money data per county

County/ place	Location	Date	Comments
Antrim	S.T. Carleton, *Heads and hearths: the hearth money rolls and poll tax returns for Co. Antrim 1660–69* (Belfast, 1991); 'An early census of Glenravel', ed. J. Smyth in *Down and Connor Historical Society's Journal*, v (1933), pp 50–5 for Glenravel; 'Hearth money roll', ed. idem in ibid., vi (1934), pp 52–4 for Aghagallon; 'Hearth money roll', ed. idem in ibid., vii (1936), pp 85–92 for Lisburn; 'The hearth money rolls for the parishes of Ramoan and Culfeightrin', ed. Frank Connolly in *J.G.A.H.S.*, i (1973), pp 10–5 for Ramoan and Culfeigh trin parishes; 'Hearth money rolls – Continued' in *J.G.A.H.S.*, vii (1977), pp 15–16 for Carncastle parish.	1666 & 1669	The focus of Carleton's work is on 1669 roll. He also indicates who in 1669 roll is also present in 1666 roll and lists 1666 names not in 1669 roll, thus providing a full listing of the 1666 tax-payers. Readers are advised to recheck the figures in appendix II rather than relying on the totals given.
Armagh	'The County Armagh hearth money rolls, A.D. 1664', ed. L.P. Murray in *Arch. Hib.*, viii (1936), pp 121–202; 'County Armagh householders, 1664–1665', ed. T.G.F. Patterson in *Seanchas Ardmhacha*, iii, no. 1 (1958), pp 96–142; 'Hearth money roll' in *J.C.L.A.S.*, vii, no. 3 (1931), pp 419–31 for barony of Orior; T.G.F. Patterson, 'Ragnall Dall Mac Domhnaill' in *J.C.L.A.S.*, x, no. 1 (1941), pp 47–8.	1664	
Cavan	Philip O'Connell, 'Historical notices of Mullagh' in *Breifny*, i, no. 2 (1921), pp 146–8 for Killinkere parish; idem, 'The parish of Lurgan and the town of	1694	

⟶

---

1 Hayes, *Manuscript sources*, v, pp 431–2; idem, *Manuscript sources … first supplement*, ii, p. 150; 'Hearth money rolls', ed. MacLysaght, pp 3–4; Carleton, *Heads and hearths*, p. 188.

County/ place	Location	Date	Comments
Cavan (cont)	Virginia' in *Breifny*, i, no. 3 (1922), pp 311–13 for Lurgan parish; idem, 'The parishes of Munterconnaught and Castlerahan' in *Breifny*, ii, no. 3 (1925–6), pp 288–9 for Castlerahan and Munterconnaught parishes; idem, 'The parishes of Crosserlough and Kildrumferton' in *Breifny*, iii, no. 1 (1927), pp 61–2 for Crosserlough parish.; 'The hearth money rolls for the baronies of Tullyhunco and Tullyhaw, Co. Cavan', ed. Francis McKiernan in *Breifne*, i, no. 3 (1960), pp 247–62 for baronies of Tullyhunco and Tullyhaw; 'Hearth money roll for the barony Castlerahan, 1664' in Breifne, vii, no. 25 (1987), pp 489–97 for barony of Castlerahan.		
Cork	Marsh's Library, MS. Z3.1.1. N.L.I., p. 1946.	1719	Account of number of houses and hearths in Cork city and liberties parishes.
		1772	See Waterford listing.
Derry	J. W. Kernohan, *The county of Londonderry in three centuries* (Belfast, 1921), pp 81–3 for Aghadowey, Desertoghill and Errigal parishes; 'Hearth money rolls (1663); City and County of Derry', ed. Diarmaid Ó Doibhlín in *Derriana: the Journal of the Derry Diocesan Historical Society* (1979), pp 41–91.	1663	The roll and an index for same.
Donegal	Alexander Lecky, *The Laggan and its Presbyterianism* (Belfast, 1905), pp 110–16 for Taughboyne (1663 and 1665), Clonleigh, Raphoe (incl. Convoy), Donaghmore, Stranorlar and Leck parishes; Hugh Deery, 'Rambles in Drumholm' in *J.C.D.H.S.*, i, no. 2 (1948), pp 107–9 for Drumhome; 'Hearth money rolls for County Donegal, 1665', ed. R. J. Dickson in *J.C.D.H.S.*, i, no. 3 (1949), pp 215–16 for Templecrone, Lettermacaward and Inishkeel parishes; 'Hearth money rolls', ed. J.C.T. Mac-Donagh in *D.A.*, ii, no. 3 (1953–4), pp 501–2 for Kilbarron, Templecarn and Inishmacsaint; 'Householders who paid hearth money tax in the year 1665' in *D.A.*, iii, no. 2 (1956),	1663 and 1665	All for 1665 unless stated.

⟶

County/ place	Location	Date	Comments
Donegal (cont.)	pp 135–6 for Inver, Killaghtee and Killymard parishes; 'Co. Donegal Hearth money rolls, 1663' in *D.A.*, iv, no. 3 (1960), pp 257 for Killybegs.; 'Hearth money rolls: Fahan' in *D.A.*, v, no. 1 (1961), pp 88–9 for Fahan.		
County Dublin	'Hearth money roll for Co. Dublin, 1664', ed. G. S. Cary in *J.K.A.H.S.*, x (1922–8), pp 245–54; 'Hearth money roll for Co. Dublin', ed. idem in *J.K.A.H.S.*, xi (1930–3), pp 386–406.	1664	Only covers parishes in County Dublin. Parishes of Clondalkin, Ballymore Eustace, Dunlavin, Rathcoole and Liberty of Donore in vol. x.
Dublin city	P.R.O.N.I., T. 808 (incomplete); *The registers of S. Catherine, Dublin: 1636–1715*, ed. Herbert Wood, v (London, 1908), pp 236–40; *The register of the Union of Monkstown (Co. Dublin): 1669–1786*, ed. Henry Seymour Guinness, vi (London, 1908), pp 85–92; *D.K.P.R.I.*, lvii (1936), pp 559–63.	1664 & 1667	New Row, St. John's Lane & Thomas St. in St. Catherine's Parish in *S. Catherine*. Monkstown union rolls for 1664 and 1666–7 in *Monkstown*. *D.K.P.R.I.* for 6+ hearths in Dublin city parishes and abstract of entire city for 1664.
Fermanagh	'Hearth-money rolls: Co. Fermanagh', ed. P. Ó Gallachair in *Clogher Record*, ii, no. 1 (1957), pp 207–14; W.H. Dundas, *Enniskillen: parish and town* (Dundalk, 1913), pp 147–8; William B. Steele, *The parish of Devenish* (Enniskillen, 1937), pp 75–6.	1665 & 1666	*Clogher Record* – Barony of Lurg, *Enniskillen: parish and town* – Enniskillen town, *parish of Devenish* – Devenish parish.
Galway city	P.R.O.N.I., T. 1023.	1724	Galway city roll. Includes data on religion of tax-payers.
Kilkenny (MS)	Carrigan's Mss, St Kieran's College, Kilkenny, vols 21 & 90.	1664	(Vol. 90). Callan town, and baronies of Ida, Kells, Knocktopher and Shillelogher. Much of Galmoy barony. (vol. 21) 559 names, of which 204 are from baronies not covered in vol. 90.
Kilkenny (published)	'The hearth money rolls of Co. Kilkenny', ed. Julian C. Walton in *Irish Genealogist*, v, no. 1 (1974), pp 33–47; 'The hearth money rolls of Co. Kilkenny', ed. idem in *Irish Genealogist*, v, no. 2 (1975), pp 169–80.	1664	Alphabetically sorted by surname.

→

County/ place	Location	Date	Comments
Kildare	*J.K.A.H.S.*, x, pp 245–54.	1664	Parts of Tipperkevin, Ballymore Eustace & Ballybought – formerly in Dublin.
Laois	Edward Ledwich, *A statistical account of the parish of Aghaboe* (Dublin, 1796), pp 46–7.	1704–94	Number of hearths taxed each year in 'Barony' of Upper Ossory for years 1704–94.
Leitrim	*Breifne*, i, p. 247 n.		Francis Mc Kiernan noted that R.V. Walker had transcribed a hearth roll for Leitrim but this has not yet been found.
Louth	'Hearth money rolls of County Louth', ed. John Garstin in *J.C.L.A.S.*, vi, no. 2 (1926), pp 79–87 for Drogheda; 'Hearth money rolls, 1663–1664', ed. idem in *J.C.L.A.S.*, vi, no. 4 (1929), pp 181–9 for rest of county; 'Hearth money rolls', ed. L.P. Murray in *J.C.L.A.S.*, vii, no. 4 (1932), pp 500–15 for Dundalk barony; Lorcán P. Ó Muireadhaigh, 'The history of the parish of Creggan in the 17th and 18th centuries' in *J.C.L.A.S.*, viii, no. 2 (1933–6), pp 152–6 for Fewes barony; Dermor MacIvor, 'Supplement to Dundalk hearth money roll' in *J.C.K.A.S.* xii, no. 4 (1952); '1666–1667 hearth money roll of Dunleer, County Louth', ed. D. Mac Iomhair in *Irish Genealogist*, iv, no. 2 (1969), pp 142–3. James B. Leslie, *History of Kilsaran* (Dundalk, 1908), pp 41–5, 127–30, 139–40, 155, 158, 192–4 for hearth rolls for various parishes.	1664 (& 1667)	Full listing of names not given for entire county – just names of some multi-hearth taxpayers. Full roll for Dundalk, Fewes and Dunlear.
Monaghan	Denis C. Rushe, *History of Monaghan for two hundred years* (Monaghan, 1996 repr.), pp 291–338.	1663 and 1665	Original lost. See Rushe, *Monaghan*, (1996 repr.), pp 360–414 for an index of the taxpayers.
Sligo	'Seventeenth century hearth money rolls with full transcription relating to County Sligo', ed. Edward MacLysaght in *Analecta Hibernica*, xxiv (1967), pp 17–89.	1663	MacLysaght describes this as a roll for 1662 (p. 3) and later as a roll for 1665 (p. 17). Most likely 1663.

→

County/ place	Location	Date	Comments
Tipperary	Thomas Laffan, *Tipperary's families* (Dublin, 1911), pp 9–193.	1665–6 and 1666–7	Roll for 1666–7 contains significantly more entries but also many transcribing errors. Also, the index is hopelessly inadequate and incomplete.
Tyrone	'Hearth-money and subsidy rolls: Co. Tyrone (Clogher diocese)', ed. P. Ó Gallachair in *Clogher Record*, v, no. 3 (1965), pp 379–86 for Tyrone Clogher parishes; 'Hearth money and subsidy rolls of the barony of Dungannon, 1666', ed. Diarmaid Ó Doibhlin in *Seanchas Ardmhacha*, vi, no. 1 (1971), pp 24–45 for Dungannon barony; John Gebbie, *Ardstraw historical survey* (Omagh, 1968), pp 21–49 for Ardstraw; 'Material for a history of the parish of Kilskerry', ed. B. O'Daly in *Clogher Record*, i, no. 1 (1953), p. 10 for Kilskeery.	1664	
Waterford	'Hearth money records' in *J.W.S.E.I.A.S*, xv, no. 2 (1912), pp 105–6.	1772	Number of taxpayers in baronies of Glenahiry, Kinnatalloon (Co Cork), Coshbride and Decies.
Westmeath	John Brady, 'The Mullingar hearth money roll, 1665' in *Franciscan College Annual* (1950), pp 59–63.	1665	Mullingar town.
	P.R.O.N.I., T. 1023.	1724?	Number of Protestants and papists in Athlone town.
Wickow	'The hearth money roll for County Wicklow', ed. Liam Price in *J.R.S.A.I.*, lxi, no. 2 (1931), pp 165–78.	1669	Abbreviated copy by Monck Mason with only householders in multi-hearth houses listed. Shilelagh and Talbotstown barony data available in summary.
	N.A.I., 7227	1739, 1748, 1779	Hearth roll summary for Co Wicklow. Houses and hearths for 1739 for parishes in Ballinacor, Shillelagh, Arklow, Newcastle and Rathdown baronies. Hearths for 1748 for Arklow, Newcastle and Rathdown parishes and hearths for Arklow parishes for 1779.
	Parishes of Dunlavin and Tober	1664	These parishes were formerly, in all or in part, in Dublin – see notes for Dublin.

APPENDIX C. TEMPLATE FOR RECORDING BAPTISMS

A suggested template for use in analysing baptisms is shown in Table 18. In the 'adjusted' columns (*adjusted first name, adjusted surname, adjusted father, adjusted mother and adjusted abode*) standardised modern spelling of the names are entered while in the 'unadjusted columns' (*first name, surname, father, mother and abode*) the exact source-data is entered. Note that the recorded date (old-style) and the historical date (new-style) are both recorded and that there are separate columns for year, month and day. The day, if not given in the baptism record, can be determined from Cheney's *Handbook of dates*.[2] The table column is a convenient reference to the appropriate table in Cheney's reference. The mother's surname column can be used if the mother's surname differs from that of the father. If the user is familiar with writing *formulae* in spreadsheets it is possible to script formulae that will automatically fill in some data based on what is entered in other cells. For instance, it is a simple task to write *formulae* that automatically enter the year, month and historical dates once the recorded date is entered.

Table 18. Template for recording baptisms.

Adjusted first name	First name	Adjusted surname	Surname	Sex	Adjusted father	Father	Adjusted mother	Mother	Mother's surname	Year	Month	Historical date	Day	Table	Recorded date	Adjusted abode	Abode	Parish
Richard	Richard	Brown	Brown	M	Thomas	Thomas	Ann	Ann		1698	Feb	1698/02/20	Sun	34	1697/02/20	NTMK	Newtown Mountkennedy	Newcastle
John	John	Jones	Jones	M	Thomas	Thomas	Jane	Jane		1698	Mar	1698/03/20	Sun	34	1697/03/20	NTMK	Newtown Mountkennedy	Newcastle
Elizabeth	Eliz	Furlong	Furlong	F	Patrick	Pat	Mary	Mary		1709	Jul	1709/07/25	Mon	34	1709/07/25			
Thomas	Tho	Ward	Ward	M	Charles	Charles	Mary	Mary		1709	Jul	1709/07/26	Tue	34	1709/07/26			
Margaret	Margrett	Nailor	Neiler	F	John	John	Elizabeth	Eliz		1710	Jan	1710/01/22	Sun	19	1709/01/22			

2 C.R. Cheney, *Handbook of dates for students of English history* (Cambridge, 1997 repr.), pp 84–155.

APPENDIX D. ESTIMATING THE PROPORTION OF FARMERS
AND LABOURERS FROM THE 1660 POLL-TAX RETURNS

In Seamus Pender's *Census of Ireland* the 'tituladoes' (gentlemen, esquires, knights and so on) in each county for which poll-tax summary data are available are listed. However, there is no information available regarding the number of labourers/cottiers/servants and farmers/yeomen who paid the tax. As the amount of tax paid by each titulado is known (*Census Ire., 1659*, pp 610–1) it is possible to use the poll-tax revenue returns (T.C.D. MS. 808, f. 275) to derive estimates for these two unknowns. As an example, the number of farmers and labourers who paid the poll-tax in County Longford is calculated.

Barony	Gents	Esqs	Baronets	Total tituladoes
Rathcleene	5	1		
Shrowell	5			
Ardagh	2	1		
Longford	4	1		
Granard	3			
Moydowe	1	1		
Total for county	20	3	1	24
Charge per titulado	4s.	10s.	30s.	
Total charge	*80s.*	*30s.*	*30s.*	*140s.*

So twenty-four titulado householders paid 140s. If we assume that 80 per cent of householders had spouses and 10 per cent had adult children then approximately forty-six (24 × 1.9) titulado persons paid appoximately 266s. (140 × 1.9). However, in the entire county 5,392 (*Census Ire., 1659*, p. 461) persons paid £338:16:00 (T.C.D. MS. 808, f. 275) or 6,776s. Thus since 46 tituladoes paid 266s. then 5,346 (5,392 − 46) persons (comprising the non-tituladoes) paid the remaining 6,510s. (6,776 − 266) tax.

Now if we define:

x := number of labourers/cottiers/servants who paid 1s.
y := number of farmers/yeomen who paid 2s.

then we can say that

$x + y = 5,346$ (number of taxpayers minus estimated number of tituladoes)

Thus, since the farmers/yeomen and labourers/cottiers/servants made up the balance of the tax payment for the county (other than the tax paid by the tituladoes) then:

$$\Rightarrow x \times (1) + y \times (2) = 6,510$$
$$\Rightarrow x + (5,346 - x) \times 2 = 6,510$$
$$\Rightarrow x + (10,692 - 2x) = 6,510$$
$$\Rightarrow x = 10,692 - 6,510$$

⇨ x = 4,182 persons (labourers/cottiers/servants) who paid 1*s*.
and
    y = 1,164 persons (farmers/yeomen) who paid 2*s*.

Now, earlier it was assumed that for each householder there were approximately 1.9 taxpayers. Thus,

    4,182 paid 1*s*. which is equivalent to approx. 2,201 householders
    and
    1,164 paid 2*s*. which is equivalent to approx. 613 householders

As the total estimate for the number of householders paying the tax in the entire county is 2,201 (labourers) + 613 (farmers) + 24 (tituladoes) = 2,838 then

    approx. 21.5 per cent of households paid 2*s*.
    and
    approx. 77.5 per cent of households paid 1*s*.

A similar exercise can be performed for any county for which there are credible poll-tax summary data and poll-tax monetary data. Thus it is possible to estimate farmer/labourer breakdown figures for Leitrim and Roscommon in Connaught, Carlow, Dublin (city and county), Kildare, Kilkenny, King's, Louth, Queen's, Westmeath and Wexford in Leinster, Cork (city), Limerick (city and county), Kerry and Waterford (city and county) in Munster and Antrim, Armagh, Derry, Down, Fermanagh and Monaghan in Ulster. Although not specified in the poll-tax ordinance merchants can be considered equivalent to gentlemen and thus required to pay 4*s*. Most counties exhibit a labourers/cottiers/servants figure of about 70–85 per cent and a farmers/yeomen figure of about 15–30 per cent.

Select bibliography

PRIMARY SOURCE MATERIAL

(For the published hearth returns see appendix B.)

'A census of Ardee, County Louth, in 1760'. Ed. Dermot MacIvor. In *Irish Genealogist*, iii, no. 5 (1960), pp 179–84.

A census of Ireland, circa 1659, with supplementary material from the poll money ordinances 1660–1661. Ed. Seamus Pender. Dublin, 1939.

'A Drogheda census list of 1798'. Ed. Moira Corcoran. In *C.L.A.H.J.*, xvii (1969–72), pp 91–6.

'A list of families around Ardee, 1766'. In *J.C.L.A.S.*, x (1941–4), pp 72–6.

'A religious census of barony of Cary 1734'. Ed. Harry Doyle. In *The Glynns: Journal of the Glens of Antrim Historical Society*, xxi (1993), pp 65–76.

'A religious census of the barony of Carey 1734'. Ed. Harry Doyle. In *The Glynns*, xxii (1994), pp 53–8.

'Archbishop Bulkeley's visitation of Dublin, 1630'. Ed. Myles V. Ronan. In *Arch.Hib.*, viii (1941), pp 56–98.

'Artrea householders, 1766'. Ed. Diarmaid Ó Doibhlin. In *Journal of the south Derry Historical Society*, i (1980/81), pp 54–61.

Begley, John, *The diocese of Limerick from 1691 to the present time* (Dublin, 1938), pp 230–3 for summary returns for diocese for 1766 and 1784.

Belmore, Earl, *The history of two Ulster manors*. London, 1881, pp 305–9 for 1660 poll-tax list for Termonmaguirk parish, County Tyrone.

Bindon, David, *An abstract of the number of Protestant and Popish families in the several counties and provinces of Ireland, taken from the returns made by the hearthmoney collectors to the hearthmoney office in Dublin in the years 1732 and 1733*. Dublin, 1736.

Burke, William, *History of Clonmel* (Kilkenny, 1983 repr.), pp 247–55 for 1661 poll-tax list for Clonmel town.

Bushe, Gervais Parker, 'An essay towards ascertaining the population of Ireland'. In *Transactions of the Royal Irish Academy*, iii (1790), pp 145–55.

Carrigan, William, *The history and antiquities of the diocese of Ossory*. 4 vols, Dublin, 1905, iv pp 404–8 for 1766 census.

Chetwood, William, R., *A tour through Ireland in several entertaining letters … interspersed with observations on the manners, customs … of that country* (1746).

Comerford, M., *Collections relating to the dioceses of Kildare and Leighlin*. 3 vols, Dublin, 1883, i, pp 269–74 for 1765 hearth tax returns and 1766 return for Kildare diocese; iii, pp 404–7 for 1765 hearth tax returns and 1766 return for Leighlin diocese.

Crosserlough, Co. Cavan 1821 census. Ed. Marie Keogh Irish genealogical sources, no. 17. Dublin, 2000.

'Desertmartin householders, 1766'. Ed. Diarmaid Ó Doibhlin. In *Journal of the south Derry Historical Society*, i, no. 3 (1982/83), pp 221–4.

Dobbs, Arthur, *An essay on the trade of Ireland*. 2 vols, Dublin, 1729–31.

Donnelly, Nicholas, *A short history of some Dublin parishes*. 19 parts, Dublin, 1907–12 contains various parish aggregate figures for houses and individuals from 1766 census – i, p. 18 for families in Donnybrook; iii, p. 105 for families and individuals (Catholics only) in Dundrum, Blackrock, Stillorgan, Kilmacud and Booterstown; iv, pp 146–7 for Monkstown union; vi, sect. 2, p. 55 for individuals in St Luke's and families in St Bridget's (St Bridget's figures seem incorrect); viii, p. 175 for individuals in St Audoen's, p. 194 for individuals in St Michael's, St John's, St Werburgh's and St Nicholas within (also p. 182 for individuals in St Michael's); ix, p. 230 for families in St James; xi, p. 58 for families in St Michan's; xiv, p. 22 for note on religious makeup of Glasnevin and Drumcondra; xv, pp 58–9 for families in Howth and families and individuals in St Doulogh's, p. 81 for families and individuals in Donabate and Portrane (Portrane figures obviously incorrect); xvii, pp 137 for individuals in Naul, Hollywood and Grallagh, p. 138 for families and individuals in Westpalstown and Ballyboghill, pp 154–5 for families in Clonmethan union.

Doyle, Harry, 'The parish of Ramoan'. Ed. Harry Doyle. In *The Glynns*, xxiii (1995), pp 55–62.

—— 'Parish of Ballintoy 1734'. In *The Glynns*, xxv (1997), pp 30–7 for 1734 religious census of Cary barony, County Antrim.

Dubordieu, John, *Statistical survey of the County of Antrim*. Dublin, 1812. Twenty-three county surveys were published by the Dublin Society in the early years of the nineteenth century. Also available are surveys for Armagh (Coote), Cavan (Coote), Clare (Dutton), Cork (Townsend), Donegal (M'Parlan), Down (Dubordieu), Dublin (Archer), Galway (Dutton), Kildare (Rawson), Kilkenny (Tighe), King's County (Coote), Leitrim (McParlan), Londonderry, Mayo (McParlan), Meath (Thompson), Monaghan (Coote), Queen's County (Coote), Roscommon (Weld), Sligo (M'Parlan), Tyrone (McEvoy), Wexford (Fraser) and Wicklow (Fraser).

'Extracts from an old census (Parish of Dunbullogue)'. Ed. Tadhg Ó Donnchadha. In *J.C.H.A.S.*, li (1946), pp 69–77.

Fahey, J., *The history and antiquities of the diocese of Kilmacduagh*. Dublin, 1893, p. 361 for 1766 census (four parishes).

Fitzgerald, J.J., 'Notes on names of inhabitants of parish of Kilmichael in 1766'. In *J.C.H.A.S.*, xxvi (1920), pp 69–79.

Flatman, Richard M., 'Some inhabitants of the baronies of Newcastle and Uppercross, Co. Dublin, *c*.1650'. In *Irish Genealogist*, vii (1986–9), pp 496–504.

—— 'Some inhabitants of the baronies of Uppercross and Newcastle, Co. Dublin, *c*.1650'. In *The Irish Genealogist*, viii (1990–3), pp 3–14, 162–74, 322–32, 498–506.

Harris, Walter. *The ancient and present state of the County of Down*. Dublin, 1744.

Howlett, J. *An essay on the population of Ireland*. London, 1786.

Hunter, R.J., 'The settler population of an Ulster plantation county'. In *Donegal Annual*, x, no. 2 (1972), pp 124–54 for Donegal muster roll of 1630.

—— and Perceval-Maxwell, M., 'The muster roll of *c*.1630: Co. Cavan'. In *Breifne*, v, no. 18 (1977–78), pp 206–22.

Laffan, James, *Political arithmetic of the population, commerce and manufactures of Ireland...* Dublin, 1785.

Ledwich, Edward, *A statistical account of the parish of Aghaboe in the Queen's County; Ireland*. Dublin, 1796.

Leslie, James B., *History of Kilsaran union of parishes in the County of Louth*. Dundalk, 1908, pp 54–5, 139–40, 158, 204 for 1731 and 1766 census materials.

—— *Armagh clergy and parishes: being an account of the clergy of the Church of Ireland in the diocese of Armagh, from the earliest period, with historical notices of the several parishes, churches, &c*. Dundalk, 1911. See notes for individual parishes for census data.

—— *Clogher clergy and parishes: being an account of the clergy of the Church of Ireland in the diocese of Clogher … with historical notices of the several parishes, churches, &c.* Enniskillen, 1929. See notes for individual parishes for census data.

—— *Derry clergy and parishes: being an account of the clergy of the Church of Ireland in the diocese of Derry … With historical notices of the several parishes, churches, etc.* Enniskillen, 1911. See notes for individual parishes for census data.

—— *Ferns clergy and parishes: being an account of the clergy of the Church of Ireland in the Diocese of Ferns, from the earliest period, with historical notices of the several parishes, churches, etc.* Dublin, 1936. See notes for individual parishes for census data.

—— *Ossory clergy and parishes: being an account of the clergy of the Church of Ireland in the diocese of Ossory, from the earliest period … With a map of the diocese and portraits of some post-disestablishment bishops.* Enniskillen, 1933. See notes for individual parishes for census data.

—— *Raphoe clergy and parishes: being an account of the clergy from the Church of Ireland in the Diocese of Raphoe, from the earliest period, with historical notices of the several parishes, churches, etc.* Enniskillen, 1940. See notes for individual parishes for census data.

—— *Ardfert and Aghadoe clergy and parishes: Being an account of the clergy of the Church of Ireland in the diocese of Ardfert and Aghadoe from the earliest period, with historical notices of the several parishes, churches, etc.* Dublin, 1940.

—— and Swanzy, Henry Biddal, *Biographical succession lists of the diocese of Dromore.* Belfast, 1933.

—— *Biographical succession lists of the clergy of diocese of Down.* Enniskillen, 1936.

MacCarthy, C.J.F., 'The people of Rathbarry in 1766'. In *Seanchas Chairbre*, no. 3 (1993), pp 44–52.

'Magherafelt householders, 1766'. Ed. Diarmaid Ó Doibhlin. In *Journal of the South Derry Historical Society*, i, no. 2 (1981–2), pp 146–52.

Maitland, W.H., *History of Magherafelt.* Draperstown, 1988 repr., pp 9–11 for 1766 census of Magherafelt.

Mason, William Shaw, *A statistical account or parochial survey of Ireland.* 3 vols, Dublin, 1914–19.

Murphy, J.E.H., 'Histories of parishes: Rathcore'. In *Meath Diocesan Magazine* (Aug. 1887), p. vi for families in Rathcore parish in 1733.

Murray, L.P., 'The history of the Parish of Creggan in the 17th and 18th centuries'. In *J.C.L.A.S.*, viii, no. 2 (1934), pp 117–62 for various censuses and tax returns.

Newenham, Thomas, *A statistical and historical inquiry into the progress and magnitude of the population of Ireland.* London, 1805.

—— *A view of the natural, political and commercial circumstances of Ireland.* London, 1809.

'Parliamentary returns for the diocese of Raphoe, 1766'. Ed. T.O.D. [Terence O Donnell?]. In *Donegal Annual*, iii, no. 1 (1954–5), pp 74–7.

'Protestant householders in the parishes of Croagh, Nantinan, Rathkeale and Kilscannell, Co. Limerick, in 1766'. In *Irish Ancestor*, ix, no. 2 (1977), pp 77–8.

Register of the church of St Thomas, Lisnagarvey, Co. Antrim, 1637–1646. Ed. Raymond Refaussé. Dublin, 1996.

Religious census of the diocese of Cloyne 1766 with other contemporary documents. Transcribed by the Rev Bartholomew O'Keeffe D.D. Ed. B. Troy. Midleton, 1998.

'Religious census of the parish of Monkstown, County Dublin, 1766'. Ed. Michael Merrigan. In *Dún Laoghaire Genealogical Society Journal*, i, no. 4 (1992), pp 157–64.

Rennison, William H., *Succession list of the bishops, cathedral and parochial clergy of the dioceses of Waterford and Lismore*. n.p., 1920, pp 233–4 for 1766 census.

'Report on the state of Popery, Ireland, 1731 (Ulster)'. In *Arch. Hib.*, i (1912), pp 10–27 for Ulster; 'Report on the state of Popery in Ireland, 1731 Munster'. In *Arch. Hib.*, ii, (1913), pp 108–56 for Munster; 'Report on the state of Popery in Ireland, 1731'. In *Arch. Hib.*, iii (1914), pp 124–159 for Connaught; 'Report on the state of Popery in Ireland, 1731'. In *Arch. Hib.*, iv (1915), pp 131–77 for Leinster.

'Royal visitation of Dublin, 1615'. Ed. Myles V. Ronan. In *Arch. Hib.*, viii (1941), pp 1–55.

Seymour, St. John D., *The succession of parochial clergy in the united diocese of Cashel and Emly*. Dublin, 1908, pp 101–2 for 1766 census.

Smith, Charles, *The antient and present state of the county and city of Waterford*. Dublin, 1746.

—— *The ancient and present state of the county and city of Cork*. 2 vols, Dublin, 1750.

—— *The antient and present state of the county of Kerry*. Dublin, 1756.

South, Captain, 'An estimate of the number of people that were in Ireland, January 10th 1695'. In *Philosophical Transactions of the Royal Society of London*, xxii (1700), p. 520.

'The 1766 religious census, Kilmore and Ardagh'. Ed. Terence P. Cunningham. In *Breifne*, i, no. 4 (1961), pp 357–62.

'The 1766 religious census for Lucan'. Ed. Mihail Dafydd Evans. In *J.C.K.A.S.*, xviii, no. 1 (1992–93), p. 101.

'The 1766 religious census for some County Louth parishes'. Ed. Tomás Ó Fiaich. In *J.C.L.A.S.*, xiv, no. 2 (1958), pp 103–17.

'The 1766 religious census for some County Tyrone parishes'. Ed. Tomás Ó Fiaich. In *Seanchas Ardmhacha*, iv, no. 1 (1960–1), pp 147–70.

'The census of 1766'. Ed. T.U. S. [Thomas U. Saidlear?]. In *J.C.K.A.S.*, vii (1912–14), pp 274–6 for 1766 census of Ballycommon, County Offaly.

The Civil Survey: A.D. 1654–6. County of Tipperary: eastern and southern baronies, i. Ed. Robert C. Simington. Dublin, 1931.

The Civil Survey: A.D. 1654–6. County of Tipperary: western and northern baronies, ii. Ed. Robert C. Simington. Dublin, 1934.

The Civil Survey: A.D. 1654–6. Counties of Donegal, Londonderry and Tyrone, iii. Ed. Robert C. Simington. Dublin, 1937.

The Civil Survey: A.D. 1654–6. County of Limerick, iv. Ed. Robert C. Simington. Dublin, 1938.

The Civil Survey: A.D. 1654–6. County of Meath, v. Ed. Robert C. Simington. Dublin, 1940.

The Civil Survey: A.D. 1654–6. County of Waterford, vi. Ed. Robert C. Simington. Dublin, 1942.

The Civil Survey: A.D. 1654–6. County of Dublin, vii. Ed. Robert C. Simington. Dublin, 1945.

The Civil Survey: A.D. 1654–6. County of Kildare, viii. Ed. Robert C. Simington. Dublin, 1952.

The Civil Survey: A.D. 1654–6. County of Wexford, ix. Ed. Robert C. Simington. Dublin, 1953.

The Civil Survey: A.D. 1654–6. Miscellanea, x. Ed. Robert C. Simington. Dublin, 1961.

The compleat Irish traveller containing a general description of the most noted cities, towns, seats buildings, loughs &c in the kingdom of Ireland. 2 vols, London, 1788.

The economic writings of Sir William Petty together with the observations upon the bills of morality. Ed. Charles Henry Hull. 2 vols, Cambridge, 1899.

Irish builder, xxxv, no. 801 (1 May 1893), pp 108–9.

The letters of Lord Chief Baron Edward Willes to the earl of Warwick 1757–1762, an account of Ireland in the mid-eighteenth century. Ed. James Kelly. Aberystwyth, 1990.

'The Popish inhabitants of the half barony of Ikerrin in 1750'. In *Irish Genealogist*, iv, no. 6 (1973), pp 578–83.

The register of the Union of Monkstown (Co. Dublin): 1669–1786. Ed. Henry Seymour Guinness, vi, London, 1908, pp 93–7 for 1766 census for Monkstown union.

'The royal visitation of Cork, Cloyne, Ross, and the College of Youghal'. Ed. Michael A. Murphy. In *Arch. Hib.*, ii (1913), pp 173–215.

'The royal visitation, 1615. Diocese of Killaloe'. Ed. Michael A. Murphy. In *Arch. Hib.*, iii (1914), pp 210–26.

'The royal visitation, 1615. Dioceses of Ardfert' [and Aghadoe]. Ed. Michael A. Murphy. In *Arch. Hib.*, iv (1915), pp 178–98.

'The subsidy roll of county Waterford'. Ed. Julian Walton. In *Analecta Hibernica*, xxx (1982), pp 95–6 for listing of available subsidy rolls.

The Synge letters. Ed. Marie-Lousie Legg. Dublin, 1996.

Tighe, William. *Statistical observations relative to the county of Kilkenny made in the years 1800 & 1801*. Dublin, 1802, pp 455–61 for 1731, 1799 and 1800 census data.

Trimble, W. Copeland, *The history of Enniskillen*. 3 vols, Enniskillen, 1919, i, pp 200–21 for Fermanagh muster roll of 1630.

Twiss, Richard, *A tour in Ireland in 1775*. Dublin, 1776.

View of the present state of Ireland containing observations upon the following subjects, viz. ... effect of the present mode of raising the revenue ... (1780).

'Visitatio regalis, 1615. Cashel and Emly'. In *Arch. Hib.*, i (1912) pp 282–311.

Wakefield, Edward, *An account of Ireland statistical and political*. 2 vols, London, 1812.

Watson's Triple Almanac (1748), p. 26; (1751), p. 28; (1753), p. 28; (1757), p. 31; (1763), p. 30.

Werburton, J., Whitelaw, J. and Walsh, Robert, *History of the city of Dublin from the earliest accounts to the present time*. 2 vols, London, 1818.

Whitelaw, James, *An essay on the population of Dublin*. Dublin, 1805. Facsimile reprint in Richard Wall (ed.), *Slum Conditions in London and Dublin*. n.p., 1974.

SECONDARY SOURCE MATERIAL

General Demographic Studies

Clarkson, L.A., 'Household and family structure, in Armagh City, 1770'. In *Local Population Studies*, no. 20 (1978), pp 14–31. The census on which this study is based is probably deficient.

Collins, J.T., 'The population of Ireland under Cromwellian rule'. In *J.C.H.A.S.*, xlvii (1942), pp 128–32.

Connell, K.H., *The population of Ireland, 1750–1845*. Oxford, 1950.

Cullen, L.M., 'Population trends in seventeenth–century Ireland', in *Economic and Social Review*, vi, no. 2 (1975), pp 149–65.

—— *An economic history of Ireland since 1660*. London, 1987.

Demos, John, *A little commonwealth: family life in Plymouth colony*. Oxford, 1970.

Daultrey, Stuart, Dickson, David and Ó Grada, Cormac, 'Eighteenth-century Irish population: new perspectives from old sources.' *The Journal of Economic history*, xli, no. 3 (1981), pp 601–28.

Dickson, David, 'The 1732 religious returns and the evolution of Protestant Kerry'. In *Journal of the Kerry Archeological and Historical Society*, xix (1986), pp 65–72.

—— 'The gap in famines: A useful myth?' in E. Margaret Crawford (ed.), *Famine: the Irish experience 900–1900*. Edinburgh, 1989, pp 96–111.

—— 'The demographic implications of Dublin's growth, 1650–1850'. In Richard Lawton and Robert Lee (eds), *Urban population development in western Europe from the late-eighteenth to the early-twentieth century*. Liverpool, 1989, pp 178–89.

—— Ó Gráda, Cormac and Daultry, Stuart, 'Hearth tax, household size and Irish population change 1672–1821'. In *Proceedings of the Royal Irish Academy*, lxxxii, C, no. 6 (1982), pp 125–81.

Doolittle, Ian G., 'Age at baptism: further evidence'. In Michael Drake (ed.), *Population studies from parish registers. A selection of readings from local population studies*. Derbyshire, 1982, pp 65–8.

Drake, Michael, 'An elementary exercise in parish register demography'. In *Economic History Review*, xiv (1962), pp 427–45 – a good introduction to parish record analysis.

—— 'The Irish demographic crisis of 1740–1'. In T.W. Moody (ed.), *Historical Studies, VI*. London, 1968, pp 101–24.

—— (ed.), *Population studies from parish registers*.

Fagan, Patrick, 'The population of Dublin in the eighteenth century with particular reference to the proportion of Protestants and Catholics'. In Alan Harrison and Ian Campbell Ross (eds), *Eighteenth-century Ireland*, vi (1991), pp 121–56.

—— *Catholics in a Protestant country: the papist constituency in eighteenth century Dublin*. Dublin, 1998. Chapter one, entitled 'The population of Dublin in the eighteenth century with particular reference to the proportion of Protestants and Catholics' (pp 9–52) is a rework of his essay published in *Eighteenth-century Ireland* (1991).

Glass, D.V., *Numbering the people. The eighteenth-century population controversy and the development of census and vital statistics in Britain*. Farnborough, 1973. Useful essays concerning the scope of and the participants in the 'population controversy' in Britain and particularly pp 53–65 for Price's and Howlett's contributions.

—— and Eversley, D.E.C., *Population in history. Essays in historical demography*. London, 1965. The essays in part ii are particularly worthwhile, especially Eversley's survey of Worcestershire.

—— and Taylor, P.A.M., *Population and emigration*. Dublin, 1976.

Graham, Tommy, 'Whitelaw's 1798 census of Dublin'. In *History Ireland*, ii, no. 3 (1994), pp 10–15.

Greven, Philip F., *Four generations: population, land and family in colonial Andover, Massachusetts*. Cornell, 1970.

Gurrin, Brian, *A century of struggle in Delgany and Kilcoole. An exploration of the social implications of population change in north-east Wicklow 1666–1779*. Dublin, 2000.

Hardinge, W.H., 'Observations on the earliest known manuscript census returns of the people of Ireland'. In *Transactions of the Royal Irish Academy*, xxiv, no. 2 (1867), pp 317–28.

Herlan, Ronald W., 'Age of baptism in the London parish of St Olave, Old Jewry, 1645–1667'. In Drake (ed.), *Population studies from parish registers*, pp 55–61.

Johnston, John, 'Settlement patterns in County Fermanagh, 1610–1660'. In *Clogher Record,* x, no. 2 (1980), pp 199–214.

Kennedy, Liam, Miller, Kerby A. with Graham, Mark, 'The long retreat: Protestants, economy and society, 1660–1926'. In Raymond Gillespie and Gerard Moran (eds), *Longford: essays in county history*. Dublin, 1991, pp 31–61.

Kussmaul, Ann, *A general view of the rural economy of England 1538–1840*. Cambridge, 1990.

Lee, J.J. (ed.), *The population of Ireland before the 19th century*. n.p., 1973. Contains reprints of J. Howlett, 'An essay on the population of Ireland' (London, 1786); (partial reprint of) Gervais Parker Bushe, *An essay towards ascertaining the population of Ireland*. In *Transactions of the Royal Irish Academy*, iii (1790), pp 145–55; William Shaw Mason, *Survey, valuation, and census of the barony of Portenehinch*. Dublin, 1821; Newenham. *A statistical and historical inquiry into the progress and magnitude of the population of Ireland*.

—— 'On the accuracy of the pre-Famine Irish censuses'. In J.M. Goldstrom and L. A. Clarkson (eds), *Irish population, economy and society*. Oxford, 1981, pp 37–56.

Le Roy Ladurie, Emmanuel, *The peasants of Languedoc*. Illinois, 1976, trans. by John Day. A masterpiece of demographic analysis.

Lockridge, Kenneth A., *A New England town. The first hundred years*. New York, 1985.

Macafee, William, 'The colonisation of the Maghera region of South Derry during the seventeenth and eighteenth centuries'. In *Ulster folklife*, xxiii (1977), pp 70–91.

—— 'The population of pre-Famine Ulster: evidence from the parish register of Killyman'. In P. O'Flanagan, P. Ferguson and K. Whelan (eds), *Rural Ireland: modernization and change*. Cork, 1987, pp 146–61.

—— 'The population of County Tyrone, 1600–1991'. In Charles Dillon and Henry A. Jefferies (eds), *County Tyrone: history and society*. Dublin, 2000, pp 433–59.

Macafee, William and Morgan, Valerie, 'Population in Ulster, 1660–1760'. In Peter Roebuck (ed.), *Plantation to partition*. Belfast, 1981, pp 46–63.

—— 'Mortality in Magherafelt, County Derry, in the early eighteenth century reappraised'. In *I.H.S.*, xxiii (1982–83), pp 50–60.

McCallum, Donald M. 'Age of baptism: further evidence' in Drake (ed.), *Population studies from parish registers*, pp 62–4.

McCoy, Gerard, '"Patriots, Protestants and Papists": religion and the ascendancy, 1714–60'. In *Bullán: an Irish studies Journal*, i, no. 1 (1994), pp 105–18.

Morgan, Valerie, 'The Church of Ireland registers of St. Patrick's, Coleraine, as a source for the study of a local pre-Famine population'. In *Ulster folklife*, xix (1973), pp 56–67.

—— 'Mortality in Magherafelt, County Derry, in the early eighteenth century'. In *I.H.S.*, xix, no. 74 (1974), pp 125–35.

—— 'A case study of population change over two centuries: Blaris, Lisburn 1661–1848'. In *Irish Economic and Social History*, iii (1976), pp 5–16.

—— and Macafee, William, 'Irish population in the pre-Famine period: evidence from County Antrim'. In *Economic History Review*, xxvii (1984), pp 182–96.

Simington, Robert C. A, '"Census"' of Ireland, *c.*1659 – the term "Titulado"'. In *Analecta Hibernica*, xii (1943), pp 177–8.

Smyth, William J., 'Society and settlement in seventeenth-century Ireland: the evidence of the "1659 Census".' In William J. Smyth and Kevin Whelan (eds), *Common ground: essays on the historical geography of Ireland*. Cork, 1988, pp 55–83.

—— 'Property, patronage and population – reconstructing the human geography of mid-seventeenth century County Tipperary'. In William Nolan (ed.), *Tipperary: history and society*. Dublin, 1985, pp 104–38.

Thomas, Colin, 'The city of Londonderry: demographic trends and socio-economic characteristics 1650–1900'. In Gerard O'Brien (ed.), *Derry/Londonderry: history and society*. Dublin, 1999, pp 359–78.

—— 'Family formation in a colonial city: Londonderry, 1650–1750'. In *Proceedings of the Royal Irish Academy*, 100 C, no. 2 (2000), pp 87–111.

Wood, Herbert. 'Methods of registering and estimating the population of Ireland before 1864', in *Journal of the Statistical and Social Inquiry Society of Ireland*, vol. 12 Part lxxxix (1909), pp 219–29.

Wrigley, E.A. and Schofield, R.S., *The population history of England 1541–1871: a reconstruction*. Cambridge, 1989.

Guides

Begley, Donal F. (ed.), *Irish genealogy: a record finder*. Dublin, 1981.

Cheney, C.R., *Handbook of dates for students of English history*. Cambridge, 1997 repr.

Dooley, Terence, *Sources for the history of landed estates in Ireland*. Dublin, 2000.

Graham, Alan, *Teach yourself statistics*. London, 1999.

Grenham, John, *Tracing your Irish ancestors: the complete guide*. Dublin, 1992.

Helferty, Seamus and Refaussé, Raymond, *Directory of Irish archives*. Dublin, 1993.

Maxwell, Ian, *Tracing your ancestors in Northern Ireland: a guide to ancestry research in the Public Records Office of Northern Ireland*. Belfast, 1997.

—— *Researching Armagh ancestors: a practical guide for the family and local historian*. Belfast, 2000.

—— *Researching Down ancestors: a practical guide for the family and local historian*. Belfast, 2001.

McCarthy, Tony and Cadogan, Tim, *Tracing your Cork ancestors*. Dublin, 1998.

Refaussé, Raymond, *Church of Ireland records*. Dublin, 2000.

Reid, Noel (ed.), *A table of Church of Ireland parochial records and copies*. Naas, 1994.

Rowntree, Derek, *Statistics without tears: an introduction for non-mathematicians*. London, 2000.

Ryan, James G., *Irish records: sources for family and local history*. Salt Lake City, 1997.

—— *Irish Church records*. Salt Lake City, 1992.

—— and Smith, Brian, *Tracing your Dublin ancestors*. Dublin, 1988.

Vaughan, W.E. and Fitzpatrick, A.J. (eds), *Irish historical statistics: population, 1821–1971*. Dublin, 1978.

Walsh, Paddy, 'Index to agricultural census, Co. Antrim 1803' (unpublished, 1993) (available in National Archives on reading room shelves).

Walton, Julian (ed.), 'The subsidy roll of County Waterford'. In *Analecta Hibernica*, xxx (1982), pp 49–96.

Miscellaneous Sources

Aalen, F., Whelan, Kevin and Stout, Matthew (eds.), *Atlas of the rural Irish landscape*. Cork, 1997.

Dickson, David, *Arctic Ireland: the extraordinary story of the Great Frost and forgotten famine of 1740–41*. Belfast, 1997.

Dillon, Charles and Jefferies, Henry A. (eds), *Tyrone: history and society*. Dublin, 2000.

Ellison, C.C., *Some aspects of Navan history*. Drogheda, 1964.

Gillespie, Raymond (ed.), *Cavan: essays on the history of an Irish county*. Dublin, 1995.

Hannigan, Ken and Nolan, William (eds), *Wicklow: history and society*. Dublin, 1994.

Moody, T.W., *Londonderry plantation*. Belfast, 1939.

O'Brien, Gerard (ed.), *Derry/Londonderry: history and society*. Dublin, 1988.

Ó Gráda, Cormac, *Ireland, A new economic history 1780–1939* (Oxford, 1994).

——, 'Liam or Jason? What's in a name?' In *History Ireland*, vii, no. 2 (1999), pp 38–41.

Pilsworth, W.J., 'Census or poll-tax'. In *J.R.S.A.I.*, lxxiii (1943), pp 22–4.

Sources for the study of local history in Northern Ireland. Belfast, 1968.

Williams, Glyn and Ramsden, John, *Ruling Britannia: a political history of Britain 1688–1988*. London, 1990.